ARK ROYAL
A FLAGSHIP FOR THE 21st CENTURY

BATTLE HONOURS

ARMADA	1588
CADIZ	1596
DARDANELLES	1915
NORWAY	1940
SPARTIVENTO	1940
MEDITERRANEAN	1940-41
'BISMARK'	1941
MALTA CONVOYS	1941

FOREWORD BY THE COMMANDING OFFICER
CAPTAIN DG SNELSON ROYAL NAVY

The start of a new commission in any of Her Majesty's Warships is something special, but the start of a new commission for HMS ARK ROYAL is something really special. For those of us privileged to serve in ARK ROYAL, what is unique is the way in which ARK's name invokes pride, enthusiasm and a sense of tremendous naval inheritance.

This ARK ROYAL (the fifth to bear the name) was last at sea in 1994 helping to bring peace to the Balkans. Her prolonged period in reserve, followed by a major upgrade and refit, means that she is now ready to serve in the new era of expeditionary warfare until Britain's new aircraft carriers come into service in the next decade. ARK ROYAL is now a significant part of Britain's capability to bring about peace and security in the world.

What is particularly special about ARK ROYAL is, of course, her people. Their enthusiasm, professionalism and pride are what bring the ship alive and make her a potent weapon in the nation's armoury. But of course it is not just the Ship's Company who contribute to the life of the ship. Many people throughout Britain, in MOD departments, engineering and manufacturing companies and support contractors, all help to make ARK what she is. Worthy of special mention is the contribution made by Babcock Rosyth Defence Ltd in the two-year refit from May 1999 to November 2001. The company's hard work, professional approach and genuine care for the ship have done so much to bring ARK alive and set her up for her new commission.

As you read this book reflect on the contribution that our predecessors made to the safety and security of Britain and the continuing contribution that people from all walks of life make, through their work with ARK ROYAL, in the service of their country.

Ark Royal
A Flagship for the 21st Century

Published by HMS Ark Royal

Edited, designed and produced by Catchline PR and Communications, Fife, Scotland

Printed by The Print House Edinburgh, Scotland

Front page: *A Sea Harrier from 800 Squadron takes off from ARK ROYAL for the first time since her refit.*

This page: *ARK ROYAL after her extensive refit at Rosyth Dockyard.*

Back page: *ARK ROYAL makes a ceremonial entrance into Portsmouth with a fly-past by a Merlin.*

CONTENTS

INTRODUCTION

I was very flattered to be asked by HMS ARK ROYAL to help in the writing of a book to mark the rededication of the ship after her extensive Rosyth refit. Thanks to the generous hospitality of the ship, I have watched with wonder as a building site was converted back into a shining aircraft carrier. Having sailed in the ARK in her previous commission, I was especially interested in the extensive modifications that make the ARK ROYAL of 2001 almost a new warship, with greatly enhanced capabilities. This book is, in part, based on the privately published book that was produced to mark the decommissioning of the ship in 1994. This was written on board ARK as she cruised operationally in the Adriatic in support of UNPROFOR. It was based on the documents held on board, the reports of proceedings and the archive built up by the ship over the years. It was also written to the background of Sea Harriers taking off fully armed on operational missions. This work did not receive a wide audience and it had been suggested I produce a new edition. I was especially happy, therefore, to be able to do this in a fully updated form as a response to a request from the ship, which wanted a rededication publication. The original text has been thoroughly revised and three new chapters added, one on the refit, prepared by Marjory Wood of Catchline PR and Communications, one on the ship post-refit and a final piece on the future. This chapter was written by myself after interviews with Rear Admiral Ian Forbes (Flag Officer Surface Flotilla), Commodore Chris Clayton RN (Commodore Naval Aviation) and Captain Richard Hawkins RN (Joint Force Harrier Staff Officer), and subsequently edited by Commander James Humphrys RN, the current Commander of HMS ARK ROYAL.

I would like to express my thanks to the staff of the Fleet Air Arm Museum, who made picture research a real pleasure, and finally to the Ship's Company of HMS ARK ROYAL, who have always made me most welcome in their midst, and with whom I hope to maintain a close relationship as the ship adds yet more pages to her already famous story.

Eric Grove
University of Hull

1
A FAMOUS NAME

Nowadays ARK ROYAL is one of the most famous names in the Royal Navy but it was not always so. For most of the Navy's history the name was considered as antique as some of the other more picaresque names of the Tudor Navy, such as ELIZABETH JONAS or WHITE BEAR, two contemporaries of the first ARK. This ship was ordered by Sir Walter Raleigh at Deptford in 1586 and was launched there on 12 June the following year by which time Sir Walter had sold her to the crown for £5,000. She thus became ARK ROYAL rather than ARK RALEIGH, although her old name seems to have stuck for some time. 'Her Majesty's good ship the ARK' was a large and powerful ship by the standards of her day and an excellent sailer and sea boat. She was 100 ft long at the keel and 37 ft in beam and was rated at 692 tons, the number of notional standard barrels that could be fitted into her hold. Her main cargo was, however, a heavy armament of 38 brass muzzle loading guns, eight short barrelled, heavy-shotted demi-canon and canon periers, 12 long-barrelled 18-pdr culverins, 12 9-pdr demi-culverins and six small 6-pdr sakers.

The Lord Admiral, Howard of Effingham, chose the powerful ARK as his flagship from which to lead the entire

The first ARK ROYAL. (Fleet Air Arm Museum)

Navy of England against the invading Armada of 1588. Howard liked ARK and used her again in 1596 when he and the Earl of Essex mounted a successful counter invasion of Spain that took and looted Cadiz. Her original owner, Sir Walter Raleigh, was back on board in 1597 when the Spanish tried another invasion attempt that was worsted by the weather. In the custom of the time ARK ROYAL was given a complete rebuild in 1608 and there was probably little of the

ARK ROYAL leads the Navy of England against the Spanish Armada off Fowey.
(E J Grove collection)

ARK ROYAL II, Britain's first ship built to operate aircraft.

old ship left when she was re-launched as the ANNE ROYAL, named in honour of the daughter of the new King, James I. In her new guise the ship was involved as the flagship of Lord Wimbledon in the disastrous 1625 expedition against Cadiz which was devastated by disease. The ship lasted into the reign of Charles I but shared the ill-luck of her new Royal owner, being damaged beyond repair by going aground in the Thames in 1636.

The name was forgotten, except by historians, until Winston Churchill became First Lord of the Admiralty in 1911. This most historically minded of First Lords fought a running battle with King George V over names for the super-dreadnought battleships being built at the time. Churchill wanted PITT, OLIVER CROMWELL and ARK ROYAL. The King would have none of it. Churchill was forced to choose a less high profile ship to carry the name and the opportunity offered itself when an aircraft carrier was being considered for the new-found Naval wing of the Royal Flying Corps, or Royal Naval Air Service as it was soon to become. A more permanent replacement for the RNAS's first ship, the converted cruiser HERMES, was being sought after HERMES' success as a seaplane carrier in trials and manoeuvres in 1913. A collier under construction at Blyth was purchased in May 1914 for conversion to an aircraft carrier. She was to be named ARK ROYAL.

The new ship displaced 7,400 tons and was radically redesigned for her new role before being launched on 5 September 1914, one month into the First World War. Only the keel and framing of the original merchantman remained: the rest of the ship was a specialised carrier. She was commissioned on 9 December and had a large internal hangar that could stow three large and three small seaplanes and four single-seat landplanes. Her original group comprised a Short seaplane with a long-range radio set, two Wight 'pusher' seaplanes, three small Sopwith seaplanes (two convertible into landplanes) and four fast Sopwith Tabloid single seater landplanes. The seaplanes were hoisted up to the long forecastle deck by crane where the wings of the larger machines were spread; they were then lifted into the water by one of two prominent steam cranes. The landplanes could be flown off the deck but had to ditch on recovery if no land base was available.

The new ARK was well equipped with workshops but was woefully deficient in speed: her 3,000 hp triple expansion engine and single screw gave only 12 knots maximum, a figure that was much reduced if heavier seas caused pitching or rolling. This limited the utility, not only of her long flight deck, but also her whole operational potential. All ARK could do was act as a relatively static aircraft base ship; fast cross-channel steamers and an old Atlantic liner had to be pressed into service as more mobile carriers.

On completion, the second ARK ROYAL was sent to the Mediterranean to support the Dardanelles operations. She earned the ship's third battle honour after Armada and Cadiz in the support given by aircraft to the ill-fated attempt to open the way to Constantinople. Her aircraft spotted for battleships' guns, scouted and carried out nuisance raids with bombs and darts. She spent most of her time around Tenedos and Rabbit Island but moved off Anzac beach when the first troop landings took place. The arrival of German submarines forced her to withdraw to the protected anchorage at Kephalo Bay on 9 May, although they gave a new role to ARK's aircraft which began to fly anti-submarine patrols. It proved impossible to operate her landplanes and ARK ROYAL's air group became an all seaplane one; by May it comprised two Shorts, two Wights, two Sopwiths and two Sopwith Schneider single seaters. Because of the difficult sea conditions at Kephalo most flights were made from a shore station set up close by at Aliki Bay.

ARK's maintainers were hard pressed to keep the flimsy and unreliable aircraft operational. In July 1915 for example, there was only one propeller between each pair of Shorts and Schneiders, the four most useful aircraft. The Wight Seaplanes were both cannibalised for spares. Local initiative was at a premium. Despite a lack of proper supplies, that had been on order for over two months, photographs were regularly being taken of Turkish positions. Techniques were developed to use photography to make gunnery spotting much more efficient. In August ARK ROYAL became the flagship for the RNAS in the Eastern Mediterranean with the arrival of Colonel Sykes, a cavalryman and former RFC officer (and future Chief of the Air Staff) with a temporary commission as both Colonel Royal Marines and Wing Captain RNAS. Effectiveness was greatly improved by ARK's group being reinforced by new Short seaplanes. In September ARK's flying programme was being maintained by three of these reliable aircraft (two more had arrived by the following month). The two Schneiders that remained still suffered from chronic engine difficulties but their speed made them useful for photo reconnaissance.

At the end of October the ship received orders to move to Mudros and Port Iero. The Aliki base was dismantled and the gear removed to the ship. The new base at Port Iero was very smooth and excellent for seaplane operations. ARK's Shorts attempted an armed reconnaissance of Smyrna but engine and bomb rack trouble frustrated the operations. ARK was then dispatched to Salonika where an Anglo-French force had been established ashore in an effort to support the Serbs being attacked by the Austrians and Germans from the north and the Bulgarians from the east. The situation was confused by the pro-Allied Greek Prime Minister, who had invited the Allies in, being deposed by the pro-German King. In a complex Balkan situation that would have echoes three quarters of a century later, ARK ROYAL's seaplanes examined the Greek defences in case the locals should offer opposition. ARK's air group was the only British air power in the area; by December it consisted entirely of six Short seaplanes.

ARK remained off Salonika until March 1916. She then returned to Mudros where, despite the Dardanelles withdrawal, she had useful duties as the base ship for the aircraft supporting the still considerable British naval presence in the Aegean. In April 1918 she moved to Syra but in October moved to Piraeus where she was at the end of the war. ARK returned to Mudros on the last day of 1918.

In April 1918 ARK ROYAL's seaplanes metamorphosed into RAF machines with the creation of the new service. In fact the Royal Naval Air Service had always been as much an autonomous air force as a part of the Navy. ARK's first commanding officer, RH Clark Hall, is listed in contemporary documents as 'Acting Commander RN and Squadron Commander RNAS'. He was promoted on 1 January to 'Commander RN and Wing Commander RNAS'. Officers with distinguished flying careers in the RAF then began their new careers in the second Ark. Among them was one Flight Lieutenant Sholto Douglas, who "had joined the air service almost from school" and would later lead RAF Fighter Command during the Second World War, subsequently becoming a Marshal of the Royal Air Force. He was not the only future Air Marshal to serve in the ship. One of their fellow aircrew was Flight Sub Lieutenant Edward H Dunning who had been invalided out of the Navy as a midshipman and had gone to Yale. He was described as having acquired there "some of the Yankee push", a factor perhaps in his immortal achievement in 1917 after he had been promoted and transferred to FURIOUS, where he became the first pilot to land on a ship under way. In 1919 ARK moved into the Black Sea to support the Allied intervention forces and White Russians against the Bolsheviks. The next few years saw her in the role of aircraft transport carrying twelve DH9s to fight the 'Mad Mullah' in Somaliland; she then had a squadron of partially-crated Bristol Fighters to confront the Turks at Chanak in 1922.

After refit at Malta, ARK was back in Turkish waters operating Fairey IIID seaplanes until the crisis with Turkey wound down. She then returned home in 1923 to become

ARK ROYAL in a previous Balkan crisis; three Fairey IIID seaplanes being hoisted out of the hold on to the foredeck ready to fly off Chanak.

depot ship for the flying boat development unit followed by a period in reserve. Recommissioned in 1928 for catapult trials, she was still in this role when she was renamed PEGASUS at the end of 1934. Under her new name she had a remarkably long and active life, seeing operational service as a fighter catapult ship defending convoys in World War Two. Sold into mercantile service as the ANITA I she finally succumbed to the cutter's torch in 1950.

The reason for the change of name in 1934 was the decision to promote the name ARK ROYAL to that of the Royal

There is nothing new in 'Jointery'; ARK ROYAL's officers during the Chanak crisis of 1922. At this time the RAF provided all Britain's maritime aircraft.

Navy's latest purpose built super-carrier ordered that year from Cammell Laird of Birkenhead. The new ARK was a magnificent ship, at 800 ft long the longest yet built on Merseyside. She displaced 23,000 tons and could carry 72 aircraft in a double deck hangar. In many ways she was the most advanced carrier yet built but she had two major weaknesses. British carrier operational technique now lagged behind that of the USA and Japan and the new ARK ROYAL would not be able to operate her aircraft fast enough to keep them all in the air; the new ship could only operate a maximum of 54 machines. Secondly, in the absence of radar, there was as yet no way that fighters could be effectively controlled so the new ship relied on her 16 4.5 guns and six multiple 2-pdr pom-poms to protect her from air attack. This explains why ARK ROYAL became a 'one off' and plans to reproduce her were replaced by a programme of armoured hangar ships with half the aircraft capacity.

Nevertheless, she was an impressive enough ship when she was launched by Lady Hoare, the wife of the First Lord on 13 April 1937. She commissioned on 16 November

ARK ROYAL III, recently commissioned at the end of 1938, flying the flag of Rear Admiral GC Royle, Rear Admiral, Aircraft Carriers.

1938 and embarked her first aircraft, Swordfish torpedo spotter reconnaissance aircraft of 820 Squadron on 12 January 1939. After work-up in the Mediterranean, ARK ROYAL joined the Home Fleet. An early landmark was the formal passing of her air group under full Royal Navy control with the implementation in Spring 1939 of the Inskip decision, taken two years before to end the clumsy dual Admiralty/Air Ministry system in force since the mid 1920s, and form the Fleet Air Arm as we now know it. At the outbreak of war in September 1939 ARK ROYAL was operating two squadrons of Skua dive bomber/fighters, 800 and 803 Squadrons – 18 aircraft; and three squadrons of Swordfish, 810, 820 and 821 Squadrons – 36 aircraft.

ARK was sent into the Atlantic to act as bait for U-boats and was narrowly missed by torpedoes, the escorting destroyers sinking the submarine. Back with the main fleet on 26 September, ARK ROYAL's Skuas shot down a German flying boat, the first enemy aircraft downed by British forces in the Second World War. That afternoon an attacking Keinkel III bomber narrowly missed the ship and the Germans claimed her as sunk. Their propaganda questions "Where is the ARK ROYAL?" did as much to endear the ship to the British people as any of the ships' many achievements.

For the rest of 1939 ARK ROYAL steamed 75,000 miles scouring the ocean for the pocket battleship GRAF SPEE. She never sighted the German raider but her imagined presence off the River Plate in December was a major factor in the Germans scuttling their ship. The following Spring saw ARK drawn into a role for which neither she nor her aircraft had been designed, contending with the Luftwaffe for control of the air over Norway after the German invasion in April. Her fighter complement was reinforced to 24 aircraft and her Swordfish reduced to 18. The fighter squadrons were at first 800 with 12 Skuas and 801 with six Skuas and six lumbering Rocs but the latter were soon replaced by 803 with a further dozen Skuas. The Swordfish squadrons, which carried out bombing missions ashore, were 810 and 820. It was hard and dangerous work for ARK's aircrew that culminated in a dive bombing attack on the damaged German battleship SCHARNHOST at Trondheim. Eight out of the 15 Skuas were lost. 'Norway 1940' was ARK's hardest gained battle honour.

The fall of France made ARK ROYAL a component of Vice Admiral Somerville's Force H, the new squadron set up to first neutralise and then replace the French fleet in the Western Mediterranean. ARK played a key role in the unhappy bombardment of the Mers El Kebir anchorage. Although her Swordfish could not slow down the fleeing fast battleship STRASBOURG they were able to seriously damage her sister DUNKERQUE at her moorings. After brushes with the Italian Air Force, ARK once more found herself deployed against the French, covering the ill-fated attempt to insert the Free French in Dakar. After the failure of that mission she returned to the Mersey for an overdue but brief refit.

Back in the Mediterranean with Admiral Somerville, ARK ROYAL with 30 Swordfish (810, 818 and 820 Squadrons), 12 Skuas (800 Squadron) and 12 new Fulmar fighters (803) was involved on 24 November in the Battle of Cape Spartivento when an Italian battle group tried to interfere with a convoy bound for Malta. Sadly, the Swordfish, so formidable against the Italian fleet by night at Taranto earlier that month, proved incapable of slowing it down by day and the Italians escaped. ARK was again narrowly missed by bombs but she spat back with her guns "like a great angry bee" as Somerville put it. Frustrating though it was, the convoy had been saved and another battle honour was added to ARK ROYAL's growing list.

ARK ROYAL III on her last operation, seen from the battleship Malaya, with HMS Argus, Britain's first 'through deck' carrier, in the background.

In early 1941 ARK and Force H attacked Italy itself. ARK ROYAL's Swordfish were tasked to take out a dam in Sardinia with torpedoes, bomb an oil refinery at Leghorn and the railway junction at Pisa and mine La Spezia harbour. ARK's Swordfish also spotted for the 15-inch guns of HMS RENOWN and HMS MALAYA in the bombardment of Genoa. Then it was back to the Atlantic looking for the battleships SCHARNHORST and GNEISENAU. A Fulmar caught a glimpse of the elusive German ships but a strike was not possible. April saw ARK ROYAL being used on the first of many missions to fly fighters into the beleaguered island of Malta. Her own air group also received welcome modernisation in the shape of 807 Squadron's Fulmars that replaced 800's Skuas. The new fighters came into their own covering the vital 'Tiger' convoy of tanks that was rushed to Egypt in May. The arrival of radar fitted cruisers allowed ARK's fighters to be directed with increasing effectiveness, although ARK herself never received a radar set.

Later that month Force H was called westwards to join the hunt for the battleship BISMARCK that had fought its way out into the Atlantic. Despite atrocious weather ARK's Swordfish played the key role in crippling the German capital ship by hitting her in the stern and jamming her rudder. The battleships KING GEORGE V and RODNEY finished her off.

Then it was back to the Malta run, covering supply ships and flying in aircraft. ARK's final battle honour 'Malta Convoys 1941', to add to her 'Mediterranean 1940-41', was well earned. The Germans deployed U-boats from the Atlantic to prevent reinforcement of Malta and, on 13 November, U-81 got in a shot at ARK ROYAL, which hit the carrier amidships. Despite much individual heroism the damage control was not

ARK ROYAL operates aircraft for the last time; minutes later she was torpedoed.

handled as well as it might have been and, after a long struggle, the ship capsized and sank at 0613 on 14 November, mercifully with the loss of only one man.

The sad end of ARK ROYAL III.

So famous was ARK ROYAL that the Admiralty immediately decided to allocate her name, adopted at this time by the City of Leeds which raised the enormous sum of £9,301,293 in a National Savings drive linked to replacing its adopted ship, to one of the projected 31,600-ton large armoured hangar carriers to be ordered in 1942. These ships were to combine a high degree of protection with a complement of 90 aircraft. This fourth ARK ROYAL was laid down at Cammell Laird on 3 May 1943 but higher wartime and immediate post war priorities delayed her launching, by Her Majesty the Queen (the present Queen Mother), until 3 May 1950. The new ARK was only slightly longer than the old, at 810 ft but much broader in the beam, 158 ft as against almost 95. She was the largest carrier ever built for the Royal Navy and on commissioning on 26 February 1955 displaced some 43,060 tons.

Completion had been delayed by the need to incorporate the latest modifications to operate aircraft that were developing at an unprecedentedly dynamic rate. The British had been forced into the forefront of the development of carrier operational technique as they operated high performance jets from hulls never designed for such aircraft. The new ARK ROYAL had an early version of the angled deck that had been designed by her first Commanding Officer Captain DRF Cambell. She also carried steam catapults, mirror landing aid, deck edge lift and strengthened arrester gear. Her first air group included Sea Hawk and Sea Venom fighters, Gannet ASW aircraft and Skyraiders from 849 Squadron for AEW.

ARK ROYAL's completion as a full attack carrier symbolised a major victory for the Admiralty in Whitehall where there had been those in influential positions, not least the Prime Minister Winston Churchill, who thought carriers too expensive. The Navy had fought a long, dogged and secret battle for the previous three years to make the point that carriers made it possible to play both a key role in the operations of the NATO Striking Fleet with its nuclear-armed American carriers, but also gave the most flexible form of air power that was usable in a wide range of contingencies all around the globe.

The new ARK was still not entirely suitable for modern fighters and strike aircraft and another refit had to be undertaken in 1956 to increase the angle of the deck and improve both accommodation and command facilities. She returned to service at the beginning of 1957 with her air group augmented by Wyvern strike aircraft. Still further

ARK ROYAL reborn, as seen in 1957, with Sea Hawks on the flight deck (left), and with the Forth Bridge, 22 May 1957 (below).

modifications were needed to operate the next generation of aircraft and, after another refit from 1958 to 1960, ARK ROYAL recommissioned with a new look air group of Scimitars, Sea Vixens and Whirlwind ASW helicopters (some of the latter flown by 820 Squadron). Her Scimitars were fitted to carry the 'Red Beard' nuclear bomb, meaning that British carriers could now add their own weight to the awesome power of the NATO Striking Fleet. The early 1960s, however, saw British defence policy begin to re-emphasise commitments 'East of Suez' and ARK ROYAL, previously deployed either to the Home or Mediterranean Fleets, went to the Far East in 1962. By now her ASW Whirlwind helicopters had been replaced by the gas turbine Wessex, the first deployed aboard a carrier, and her AEW aircraft were Gannets, although still carrying the same radar as the old Skyraiders. In 1963, during a brief visit home, 801 Squadron exercised their new Buccaneer strike

Britain's impressive carrier fleet at the beginning of the 1960s. ARK ROYAL is flanked by Hermes to port and Victorious to starboard.
(Fleet Air Arm Museum)

The shape of things to come: the prototype of the Harrier, the Hawker P1127, after its first deck landing on ARK ROYAL in 1963.
(Fleet Air Arm Museum)

aircraft from the ship and in 1964 the more powerful Buccaneer 2 was embarked for a week's trials. A more important trial, though it did not seem like it at the time, was when Hawker test pilot Bill Bedford landed a P1127 vertical take-off and landing (VTOL) prototype on board in 1963. At the time many in the Navy had doubts about the concept, as the performance of the little aircraft was so much less than that of classical conventional take-off and landing machines. The P1127, forerunner of the Harrier, was, however, the true shape of things to come.

For most of the mid-1960s, ARK was in the Indian Ocean or the Far East, her aircraft taking part in the confrontation with Indonesia and the imposition of the Beira Patrol through which Britain showed her displeasure at Rhodesian UDI. She was slated for relatively early withdrawal from service but then policy was put into turmoil in 1966 by the RAF's success in achieving the cancellation of the new carrier CVA01 that would have replaced ARK ROYAL. In order to retain a carrier capability into the 1970s to sustain East of Suez it was decided to rebuild ARK ROYAL with a fully angled deck, strengthened arrester gear and many other modifications to allow the operation of not only Buccaneer 2s but Phantom fighters and Sea King helicopters.

The work began in October 1966 and lasted until February 1970, costing more in cash terms, £30 million, than the original cost of the ship. Now displacing a massive 50,170 tons full load, making her the largest ever Royal Navy warship, she was recommissioned on 24 February by Queen Elizabeth the Queen Mother who still retained a strong interest in 'her' ship. By this time, further policy reviews and the abandonment of the East of Suez role made it seem as if the ship would only serve for another year or so. The focus of the

ARK ROYAL IV in the 1970s with Phantoms and Buccaneers.
(Fleet Air Arm Museum)

A Harrier GR3 of 1 Squadron (now a part of Joint Force Harrier) makes a pioneering landing on ARK ROYAL IV in October 1975. (Fleet Air Arm Museum)

ARK ROYAL IV in context as part of an air/amphibious task group in 1975: she is operating off Puerto Rico with a County class guided missile destroyer Hampshire and the amphibious transport dock Fearless. (Fleet Air Arm Museum)

ARK ROYAL IV is scrapped at Cairnryan in February 1981. (Fleet Air Arm Museum)

Royal Navy's concerns had become the Soviet Navy and the flanks of NATO and in November ARK found herself in her old haunts in the Mediterranean under the close scrutiny of an increasingly aggressive Soviet Navy. It had become practice for Soviet 'tattletales' to trail NATO carriers and ARK had attracted the attention of a KOTLIN SAM class vessel with the hull number 365. As the carrier was launching Phantoms at night the ship attempted to cut across the ARK's bows and was lucky to escape with a glancing blow. The Soviet ship owed its survival to the prompt action of Captain Ray Lygo in going full astern.

The change of Government in 1970 and the embarrassment of scrapping an asset on which so much had been spent, especially at a time of growing naval confrontation, brought a reprieve for ARK ROYAL although she would be the Navy's only attack carrier after 1971. ARK's unique status enhanced her fame still further and the 13-week television series 'Sailor' made ARK ROYAL a household name again. By the time she was eventually decommissioned in December 1978 the thought of a Royal Navy without another ARK ROYAL had become unthinkable. The very month that the old ARK paid off, a new ship of the name was ordered from Swan Hunter and laid down at the Wallsend yard. As the old carrier was towed away to be scrapped in the Autumn of 1980, the new ARK ROYAL was rapidly taking shape.

ARK ROYAL V

The origins of the current ARK ROYAL go back to the beginning of the 1960s when a new escort cruiser was designed to accompany the planned new generation of aircraft carriers. Even the largest carriers that would fit into British dockyards would be hard pressed to operate large ASW helicopters in addition to the expected high performance fixed wing types of the future. It was thought, therefore, that a cruiser type ship with a hangar and flight deck would provide a valuable complementary capability while also providing a useful extra command platform. The project was delayed by the Polaris programme, which led to two of the existing Tiger class cruisers being converted to the new role. By the time drawing office staff could be redeployed to the project in the mid to late 1960s the ship had acquired a whole new significance.

The decision to abandon large fixed wing carriers, taken in 1966, threatened to deny the Royal Navy any organic air capability beyond helicopters. The Navy's future planners made the point that this would greatly diminish the operational flexibility of the fleet but there were strong elements within the service who were anxious not to reopen the carrier controversy. The superstructure of the new design was, however, moved to the starboard side to provide a through deck to allow the operation of larger numbers of Sea Kings. The Naval Staff at the end of the 1960s, headed by a new and pro-carrier First Sea Lord, Admiral Sir Michael LeFanu, wanted the ship to operate the new Harrier short take-off and vertical landing (STOVL) fighter. The latter would be a vital asset in order to 'hack' shadowing aircraft, probe for surface targets and provide organic combat air patrol. There was no question of putting this suggestion forward as yet, however, as it would not have received support at Chiefs of Staff level.

Just before leaving office in 1970 Denis Healey, the Secretary of State who had cancelled the CVA01 carrier programme, approved the first of the new cruisers. The change of Government meant that the idea had to be sold over again to his successor, Lord Carrington. This was done, but in the context of the financial climate of the early years of the Heath Administration it was a harder job selling the idea to the Treasury. It would not be until 1 April 1973 that the first ship, HMS INVINCIBLE was ordered.

The 'through deck cruiser' was still essentially a helicopter carrier. Trials with RAF Harriers took place aboard the old ARK ROYAL in 1971 and a Naval Staff requirement was issued but against a background of financial and political instability. It was not until May 1975 and some hard advocacy by the First Sea Lord, Admiral Sir Edward Ashmore, that the Wilson Government ordered Sea Harriers for the Royal Navy. The Exocet missiles included in the original design were deleted and the ships began to be regarded more and more as aircraft carriers rather than cruisers.

The second ship of the class, ordered on 14 May 1976, received another old carrier name, ILLUSTRIOUS. The third of the class was to have been INDOMITABLE, but public outcry at the demise of the old ARK ROYAL resulted in the name being handed on to the third 'cruiser'. She was ordered on the first day of December 1978 from Swan Hunter on the Tyne and laid down on the 14th. The retention of the name was also calculated to spike the guns of the preservation lobby who were keen to keep the old ARK ROYAL in some capacity or another.

With the commissioning of INVINCIBLE in 1981, the designation aircraft carrier became official and she was dubbed a 'CVS' for 'ASW Support Aircraft Carrier'. By the time ARK ROYAL commissioned in 1984, the designator CVSA was coming into vogue, reflecting the ships' utility as attack/assault assets depending on the type of air group embarked. Latterly, however, the designation settled down as CVSG, the 'G' standing for 'Guided Missile' and reflecting retention of a Sea Dart area defence anti-air guided missile capability, a relic of the original cruiser concept.

Adding Sea Harriers to the INVINCIBLE design necessitated various modifications including fixed aircraft holdback units, extra workshop facilities and the fitting of a ski

ARK ROYAL is reborn once more at Swan Hunter on the Tyne.
(Fleet Air Arm Museum)

Fitting out ARK ROYAL at Swan Hunter.
(Fleet Air Arm Museum)

The new ship is launched on 2 June 1981.
(Fleet Air Arm Museum)

jump ramp to increase the take-off payload of the Sea Harriers. The first two ships only had seven degree ramps but ARK ROYAL was built with a full twelve degree ski jump that has since been fitted to her sisters. Her accommodation, hangar and workshop spaces were also improved.

The new ARK ROYAL was launched by Her Majesty Queen Elizabeth the Queen Mother on 2 June 1981. Her Majesty had always taken a great interest in the previous ARK which she had also launched and which she had visited as much as possible. She wished to maintain this close relationship with the new ship also. The only discordant note was struck by John Nott, the Secretary of State for Defence, who refused to give a commitment that the ship would go into service. This was in the middle of the Defence Review of that year in which it was decided to cut the CVS force to three ships. (The conventional fixed wing carrier HERMES, converted for Sea Harrier operations, was still in service at this stage.) In the event the plan adopted was to sell INVINCIBLE to Australia but this was abandoned when the Nott review was unexpectedly shelved as a result of the Falklands War which vindicated the decision to maintain a fixed wing carrier capacity. Not only was it decided to retain all three CVS hulls but extra close-in armament was added to ARK's specification. Airborne early warning (AEW) Sea King AEW2s were also added to the ARK's projected air group of Sea King HAS5 ASW helicopters (known as Sea King Jezebels, SKJs for short, because of their ability to monitor 'Jezebel' passive sonobuoys) and Sea Harrier FRS1s, the SHARs.

In accordance with contemporary policy, both types of aircraft could carry the WE177 nuclear bomb configured either for surface or underwater burst. ARK ROYAL was therefore fitted to carry these weapons although, in keeping with the policy of the time, it was never confirmed or denied that she was actually in possession of these. This later led to various demonstrations against the ship during port visits and, coupled with the extra security measures the weapons demanded, made them perhaps more trouble than they were worth. With contemporary ASW tactics evolving in ways that made nuclear weapons a positive menace to passive sonar operations, and the belated development of effective homing torpedoes, the opportunity was taken at the end of the Cold War to remove the weapons from all RN ships. This followed the US-Russian agreement of 1991 to remove similar weapons from their Navies.

ARK ROYAL was accepted into service at Portsmouth on 1 July 1985 with much fanfare. Her first commanding officer, Captain JL Weatherall, had, however, quite a task on his hands to deal with the several shortcomings of finish and

ARK ROYAL arrives at Portsmouth for the first time on 1 July 1985. (Fleet Air Arm Museum)

The first of many Sea Harrier landings. Lt Cdr Hugh Slade in an aircraft of 899 Squadron on the day ARK ROYAL arrived in Portsmouth. (Fleet Air Arm Museum)

cleanliness that were still in evidence: 140 Swan Hunter employees remained at work on the ship for the next two weeks, while the Ship's Company undertook an intensive training programme to prepare the new carrier for trials.

ARK ROYAL sailed on 15 July for an arduous programme of sea acceptance trials that included embarking three SHARs and three SKJs. She then returned to Portsmouth to be an exhibit at both Navy Days and the Royal Navy Equipment Exhibition. Swan Hunter personnel again swarmed over the ship to remedy outstanding defects. Sea acceptance trials followed in October and on 1 November the Queen Mother was present for the formal commissioning ceremony. Captain Weatherall reported that he believed ARK ROYAL was already on a firm base and that there was "much to give encouragement for the future".

The present ARK ROYAL as new on her final machinery acceptance trials.

Three days later she sailed for the Mediterranean to take advantage of the good weather to be expected there to continue her sea trials. Flying trials were carried out with two SHARs and the 12 degree ski jump proven. In general the deployment to Crete and back was a great success, not least in consolidating a strong sense of team spirit among the Ship's Company. Trials continued in home waters with a mini group of six aircraft but ARK's two designated squadrons, 801 of six SHARs and 820 of nine SKJS, did not join in toto until 24 February 1986. Having made it over the hurdle of Basic Operational Sea Training at Portland, ARK then went to the North Western Approaches in April for Air Group Work Up. A Sea Harrier was lost in these manoeuvres, happily with no loss of life. On 23 April the ship was assessed as being at a satisfactory state of operational readiness and, having landed her air group, the ship was back in Portsmouth on 24 April. The final finishing touches were made, notably the fitting of the close-in weapons systems, and the ship was formally accepted from Swan's with the reading of the Form D448 on 10 June 1986. Captain Weatherall reported on an excellent meeting with the ship's builders; it had been a reaffirmation of the "strong and happy liaison" with the company.

On 17 June 1986 ARK ROYAL sailed from Portsmouth on her first deployment. She embarked her full air group for the first time as 801 and 820 were now joined by the three AEW Sea Kings (known as 'Sea King Whiskeys' (SKWs) or more commonly the 'Bags'). This description of 849 Squadron's aircraft stems from the ungainly looking radar suspended from the side. The first task was to conduct Exercise Liberty Train, a working passage of the North Atlantic, to take part in the international naval review held at New York to mark the centenary of the Statue of Liberty.

The main war role of the ship was to command the recently redesignated ASW Striking Force (ASWSTRIKFOR) of the main NATO Striking Fleet. This redesignation reflected the new emphasis on deep field ASW allowed by the towed array. The exercise provided vital experience for, and smoothed, the interface between FOF3's command staff, the designated command for ASWSTRIKFOR, and the flagship.

Major exercises were held in the summer of 1986 to explore the ASWSTRIKFOR concept based around the year's major NATO Northern Flank exercise Northern Wedding. ARK, with most of ASWSTRIKFOR, made a fast and silent passage to the Greenland Iceland UK Gaps (the GRIUK). Emission control (Emcon) was reinforced by operational decoy (OPDEC) techniques to mask the group's presence. At the GRIUK, operations began to sanitise the area of nearby submarines to allow the passage of the following components of the Striking Fleet. SHAR availability was disappointing and put a strain on logistic support, however RFA runs to the Shetlands and an airbridge to Norway maintained Sea Harrier and Sea King availability at sufficient levels.

The operation of ASWSTRIKFOR, with assets spread out widely ahead of the Striking Fleet advancing into the Norwegian Sea, was designed to put into effect NATO's Forward Maritime Strategy. However, it placed a great strain on air defence and it proved difficult to control all anti-air warfare assets into a co-ordinated and flexible whole. The ASW operations themselves, based around the long range use of passive sensors were, however, a great success. A true picture of the underwater operational picture was maintained which was the key factor in taking on and defeating the Soviet submarine force drawn out to engage the carrier. ARK's Captain considered the ship had done well and that the exercise had shown that "we had finished the process of growing up and were a fully paid up member of the team".

November found ARK off Cornwall to disembark 820 Squadron and to pick up the Commando Sea Kings of 845. This was to work the ship up in her alternative role of interim LPH, ie helicopter assault transport. Commodore Jeremy Larken, Commodore Amphibious Warfare, joined the ship the same day, 5 November, and ARK passed up to the Clyde to pick up the First Dutch Amphibious Combat group by helicopter at Tail O' The Bank. The exercise, High Tide, demonstrated the flexibility of amphibious capability as the originally designated landing area was made impossible by wind and rain. It also highlighted the flexibility of the CVS to undertake this alternative role, although only in a 'quick dash' mode. The ship thereupon sailed round the north of Scotland and landed and recovered the troops near Arbroath. To add to the completeness of ARK's achievement, the Vulcan Phalanx gun system, which had still not been fully proven, achieved its required satisfactory grading, the last major piece of the ship's fit to do so. Captain Weatherall had brought the ship to an enviable level of operational capability.

ARK ROYAL preparing RAS fuel starboard side and stores port side, 18 February 1987.

At the beginning of 1987 ARK ROYAL was to cross the Atlantic for Exercise Caribtrain in the West Indies. The Atlantic was at its wintry worst and very heavy weather reduced the planned programme of exercise evolutions. Passing the Azores on 26 January the ship suddenly experienced flooding forward in Alpha section. The heavy seas had forced off a section of plating in the bow. The flooding was contained and the ship was able to continue to Barbados for temporary repairs. It was found that two square metres of shell plating had detached on the port side of the bow causing free flooding to the compartment. The probable cause was assessed as poor welding and inadequate stiffness of support to the plating in that area which, in turn, had led to fatigue failure. The compartment was filled with concrete alongside at Barbados between 2 and 8 February.

During this drama Captain MGT Harris, a former submariner who joined the ship from a posting on the Central Staff in the Ministry of Defence, succeeded Captain Weatherall in command on 3 February. He took the ship out on 9 February to take part in ASW exercises either side of a major FLEETEX with the United States Navy. ARK scored a notable success when her Sea Dart downed a Chukar target that had survived five American Standard Missiles. 801 Squadron was also able to demonstrate its effectiveness with 1,000 lb bombs on the Vieques bomb range.

ARK's teething troubles continued, however. On 18 March, as she was taking part in Trial Punish on the AUTEC range in the Bahamas, the port outer Olympus gas turbine failed catastrophically and spectacularly, with smashed turbine blades being projected through the uptakes onto the flight deck. The turbine was replaced at sea. ARK's bow hole had to await further attention at an emergency docking on her return to Portsmouth in late April. The repair could not be completed until the ship was docked for her major assisted maintenance period (AMP) at Portsmouth that lasted from 13 July to 18 August.

After a most successful work-up ARK ROYAL sailed on 3 November for Exercise Purple Warrior, the biggest single maritime operation for British forces since the Falklands War. It was carried out to test the ability of the United Kingdom Task Group to protect and evacuate UK nationals from a distant shore. With ILLUSTRIOUS carrying the commando helicopters in the LPH role, ARK was to act both as command ship and air defence and attack carrier (CVA), providing mobile air support with three Harrier squadrons. On 3 November the ship sailed with the 12 Sea Harriers of 800 and 801 Squadrons plus six RAF Harrier GR3s from No 1 (F) Squadron. The three AEW Sea Kings of 849B were supplemented by a fourth aircraft from 849A flight to achieve 24-hour AEW surveillance. A flight of two SKJs of 826 Squadron was also carried for helicopter delivery service (HDS), 820 having been landed at Culdrose. The staffs of both FOF3 and the Joint Forces HQ were also embarked pushing the ship's complement to about 1,460. Accommodation for the extras was arranged by converting some passageways and electrical spaces into cabins and mess decks.

Admiral Hugo White and Major General Nick Vaux arrived to join their staffs on 4 November and the ship stayed in the Channel while rehearsal landings were carried out on the South Coast. On one day alone 50 SHAR and GR3 sorties were flown. The force then proceeded to the exercise area in

ARK ROYAL entering the River Tyne circa 1988.

South Western Scotland where it arrived on the 8th. The first landings were made on the 9th and the JFHQ staff went ashore on 11 November after a forward base had been set up ashore. The SHARs provided combat air patrol (CAP) cover over both the ships and ashore while the GR3s reconnoitred the landing areas. The threat was from Buccaneers from the North West and Jaguars from the East but rules of engagement would not allow engagements until 'hostile action' commenced on the 11th. The GR3s went ashore on the 12th which, together with the departure of the Joint Forces staff, helped relieve pressure on ARK's accommodation spaces. The SHARs were kept busy defending from the Buccaneers and Jaguars and 'hacking' shadowing Nimrods. A four over four by day and two over two by night tasking was maintained and on 16 November ARK launched no less than 52 Sea Harrier sorties. With some help from RAF Phantoms, continuous cover was maintained throughout until the exercise ended.

Most of ARK's enhanced air group disembarked to Yeovilton on the 18th/19th. She had played the key role in the entire operation, despite having lost a gas turbine on 8 November, which limited her speed to 25 knots. Admiral Oswald, C-in-C Fleet, congratulated the ship on having risen to the challenge of Purple Warrior with great style. He congratulated the ship on a most successful exercise and thanked the Ship's Company "for your enthusiasm, your hard work and professionalism, for your cheerfulness in the face of some pretty bloody weather and, in sum, for your contribution to an outstanding success. Well done".

The withdrawal from East of Suez in 1971 did not mean the end of periodic naval forays out of the NATO area. Governments considered it useful to demonstrate some capacity to deploy naval forces outside the NATO area where Britain retained various defence commitments and where she wished to sell military and naval equipment. The Royal Navy was only too ready to take advantage of these opportunities to send groups of ships on deployments to provide useful training and experience of ships and their crews, to maintain links with traditional friends and, more generally, to demonstrate the service's continued global reach should circumstances demand it.

By 1988 it had been decided that the group deployment should centre on Australia's bi-centennial. ARK would lead a group out to take part in the celebrations, coming back the same way rather than continuing round the world; hence the name of the deployment Outback 88. The maximum number of visits and exercises would be crammed in during the deployment that was to take six months. Extensive preparations were required, both for the ship and her crew. Two Olympus gas turbines and a diesel generator were replaced, the flight deck was refurbished and the ship generally spruced up. Rear Admiral AP Woodhead, Flag Officer Second Flotilla, flying his flag in ARK on 13 June, commanded Outback 88. With a detachment of Royal Marines on board and her air group swelled by two Commando Sea Kings of 845 Squadron, she slipped and proceeded from Portsmouth for her long odyssey. She was carrying a total of 22 aircraft, nine SKJ Mk 5 ASW helicopters, eight SHARs and three SKWs plus the 845 flight of two. Because of the increased complement of over 1200 men, the gymnasium had been converted to a mess deck. In addition, every available space was crammed with spares and defence sales equipment. The other members of TG318.1 were the Type 42 destroyer HMS EDINBURGH, the towed array Leander Class SIRIUS and the three RFAs OLWEN, ORANGELEAF and FORT GRANGE. No sooner was the group at sea than exercises were being carried out in the Bay of Biscay with both the French Navy and the RAF in the shape of the frigate ACONIT and Super Etendard, Atlantique and Nimrod aircraft.

On 16 June ARK steamed for a quarter of an hour in close company with the liner CANBERRA, the 'great white whale' of the Falklands war. The following day Jolly Roger began, an ASW exercise that allowed the TG to shake down together and the 820 Squadron SKJs, working hard in continuous ripple mode, to practice co-operation with the towed array frigate. On the first day 801 also had trade in the shape of Spanish Matador (Harrier) and Mirage aircraft. On entering the Med, ARK's group met with an Italian task group led by the carrier GIUSEPPE GARIBALDI. A PASSEX was held in which two 801 Sea Harriers, supported by a party of maintainers, deck crew and supervisors, operated from the Italian ship. Because of the Italian Navy's legal difficulties with operating fixed wing aircraft, procurement of STOVL aircraft had been delayed for the GARIBALDI and the Italians found the experience most useful. Two days later ARK met another aviation ship, the latest Soviet large aircraft carrying cruiser BAKU. This was encountered close to the Soviet's Hammamet anchorage and the two ships sailed in company for over an hour. The Russians seemed anxious to show off their prowess in the STOVL mode of operating their normally VTOL Forgers and one of the few observed running take-offs with the type was observed.

Malta was the next port of call, the former main base of the British Mediterranean Fleet but recently out of bounds because of political differences with the Maltese government. Relations were now much better, as indicated by the planned visit, but the opposition Labour Party and its associated trade unions came out against it, given the excuse provided by ARK ROYAL's nuclear capability. A tanker was hi-jacked to block the entrance to Grand Harbour. The Task Group therefore put into St Paul's Bay to a great welcome by a flotilla of small boats full of cheering well wishers. ARK's Ship's Company were treated with both warmth and hospitality when ashore and the Maltese Prime Minister and other government officials were hosted on board. When the ship sailed on 29 June she was surrounded by another throng of well-wishers.

On 2 July ARK ROYAL anchored at Port Said for the transit of the Suez Canal that began that same day. After anchoring briefly in the Bitter Lakes the transit was completed the following day. Over 150 of the Ship's Company had taken the opportunity to sight-see in Egypt before the Task Group set off down the Red Sea. Temperatures passed the 40 degree celsius mark and the sand-laden atmosphere turned the ship's upperworks and aircraft brown. A fortuitous and rare shower of rain in the Indian Ocean eventually washed off this deposit. On 14 June the ship passed Djibouti and entered the Indian Ocean. On 16 July a major helicopter delivery service (HDS) operation was carried out using the two SKAs 'leapfrogging' from ARK via FORT GRANGE and EDINBURGH to Colombo in Sri Lanka, a total distance of 320 miles. This was an especially notable achievement as the pilots of the Commando

During the 1988 deployment ARK ROYAL visited Subic Bay in the Philippines. The RFA Olwen is in the foreground and the battleship New Jersey in the background.
(Fleet Air Arm Museum)

Sea Kings had to rely on dead reckoning for navigation.

Later in the month 820 flew off to take part in Exercise Starfish, an annual event carried out under the auspices of The Five Power Defence Arrangements of 1971. Under these Britain has obligations to consult with Australia, New Zealand, Malaysia and Singapore if the security of the latter two is threatened. Flying from the Royal Malaysian Air Force airfield at Kuantan, the Sea Kings demonstrated their active dipping sonar capability at ranges of over 100 miles from base. The target was the Australian Oberon class submarine HMAS OXLEY. While this was in progress five SHARs of 801 were flown off to Paya Lebar airfield in Singapore. They stayed from 22 July to 4 August carrying out a varied training programme with the local A4s, Hunters and F5s.

On 23 July the ship berthed at the old naval base at Sembawang, a nostalgic event for some, although the enormous and rapid development of Singapore since 1971 is impressive. While some enjoyed the sights of the island and others ventured further afield, others busied themselves with a two-week self-maintenance period assisted by a Fleet Maintenance Unit from HMS DEFIANCE in Plymouth. On 8 August the ship sailed for the Philippines and the American naval base at Subic Bay where she docked astern of the battleship USS NEW JERSEY.

ARK ROYAL proceeded to the Subic Bay Exercise Area for a demonstration of New Jersey's 16-inch guns. Two broadsides were fired with maximum flash effect. After this firework display the serious training in modern naval warfare began. USS HADDOCK, an American SSN, provided a demanding ASW target in the water conditions but SKJ co-operation with SIRIUS improved still further and the 'fighting pair' Sea King concept was vindicated. USN P3Cs also gave support. Sea Dart firing against Petrel targets was less successful and studies began on how to make it third time lucky with Sea Dart as ARK pointed her bows towards Hong Kong, carrying out a PASSEX with the Hong Kong Squadron patrol vessels on the 23rd. The ship moored alongside at HMS TAMAR later that day. After some busy days for her Ship's Company enjoying the sights of Hong Kong, ARK sailed only for an AEW Sea King to spot a drifting boat full of 26 Vietnamese boat people. They were rescued by HMS EDINBURGH, transferred to OLWEN and taken to Singapore.

Exercise Sethia Kawan, designed to test British support for the Sultan of Brunei (who jealously guards his independence from Malaysia), was the next activity. Deployed ashore were the Brunei armed forces together with troops from the British garrisons both in Brunei and Hong Kong. On 3 September the Sultan himself visited ARK. Her contributions to the exercise included landing 250 Bruneian assault troops from the ship and the SHARs carrying out reconnaissance and ground attack missions under the control of forward air controllers. Then it was another 'Five Power' Defence exercise Lima Bersatu. The aim was the integration of maritime and air forces. Two days of air operations against Malaysian and Singaporean aircraft were followed by a similar period of attack operations against land targets in both countries.

As the ship neared Australia a series of exercises

The high spot of the 1988 'Outback' deployment was the visit to Sydney. (*Fleet Air Arm Museum*)

In early 1988 ARK ROYAL exercised together with her sister HMS Illustrious.

was held with units of both the RAN and RAAF. On 21 September two 820 Squadron aircraft, and one each from the Sea King flights, disembarked to Amberley and the ship berthed at Brisbane, at Hamilton Wharf.

On 25 August, with press on board, ARK sailed for Sydney and the great 20th Anniversary Naval review, the high spot of the whole deployment. The governor of New South Wales, Sir James Rowland, embarked for the entry to Sydney Harbour. The ship was met by a mixed bag of friendly, cheering well-wishers and anti-nuclear protestors. Judicious ship handling prevented any collisions and ARK berthed safely at the Sydney cove Passenger Terminal between the Opera House and the Harbour Bridge.

The ship was soon immersed in a social and sporting programme of massive proportions: over 10,000 visitors were hosted on board. On 29 September ARK ROYAL took part in a march past of about 8,000 personnel from the international group attending the Review. The following day she took up position in the harbour and, on 1 October, the great event took place, conducted by HRH The Duke of York embarked in HMAS COOK. ARK was moored close by the NEW JERSEY and the French cruiser COLBERT, the three largest ships present. Four SHARs of 801, two Sea Kings of 820 and an SKW of 849B took part in the fly past.

ARK sailed from Sydney on 7 October after one of the most memorable visits in the ship's entire career. It was back to business with evolutions in the Jervis Bay exercise areas. The participants were the ships that had taken part in the review; from Australia, New Zealand, the Netherlands, France, Italy and Malaysia as well as TG 318.1. Two RAN Sea Kings embarked for carrier experience and 820 had considerable success in active operations against the Australian submarines ONSLOW and ORION. The high spot of SURFEX 429 on 8 October was ARK's SHARs sinking the old patrol boat HMAS BUCCANEER with 1,000 lb bombs. Air defence exercises were also held with the enemy being provided by RAAF Learjets, Macchis and F18s. The SHARs did their share of attacking and also with providing the threat for ADEXs with both the USS INGERSOLL and HMS SIRIUS. The exercises ended on 11 October and the two RAN Sea Kings returned home to Nowra. Two SHARs went ashore also for yet another air show, this one at Richmond.

The ship was bound for Melbourne but again her nuclear capability caused problems, the most serious yet. The Seamen's Union had announced a boycott of the ship and RFA FORT GRANGE and, therefore, no tugs were available. ARK remained under way in the Bay of Port Philip. The assigned berth for the carrier was alongside Princes Pier up a narrow straight channel followed by a complete 180 degree turn. This was tricky enough at the best of times without tugs but high winds ruled out an unassisted berthing completely. The ship waited three days for reason to prevail but despite the best efforts of Admiral Woodhead, supported by the RAN and the British high commissioner, the unions, supported by the State Premier, remained intransigent. ARK had no alternative but to sail away on 16 October with Freemantle in Western Australia the next port of call. Two Sea Kings were disembarked ashore to RAAF Laverton for the duration of the Melbourne stand off.

Poor weather with 60-70 knot winds added to the general gloom but flying began again on the 18th with ASW exercises against the 2058 target and exercises with RAAF P3s. On the 22nd SHARs were flown ashore for displays and the ship berthed at Freemantle the following day. Again the nuclear issue raised its ugly head and the crane drivers' union boycotted the ship. This necessitated boat transfer of personnel rather than the use of brows but the boycott was lifted on 24 November, which also happened to be the day of the visit of the Australian Defence Minister Kim Beazley. A full social and sporting programme was enjoyed by all in excellent weather and the visit was a fitting culmination to what had been, despite some glitches, a very successful six weeks.

ARK recovered those aircraft still ashore on 31 October and sailed for Bombay two days later. The Task Group kept itself busy over the following days, with surface, ASW and air defence exercises. On 15 November the ships reached Bombay and conducted Defence Export Days on the 18th and 19th; the first in harbour and the second at sea after the ship had left Bombay for Suez.

ARK was not the only carrier in the Indian Ocean in late 1988 with the Iran/Iraq war demanding the presence of an American carrier. This allowed useful exercise opportunities and on 22 November a major War At Sea exercise (WASEX) began with the USS NIMITZ. The super carrier's F14, A6, A7, S3 and E2 aircraft provided a formidable 'threat' and valuable insights into the 'WAS' tactics of the US Navy. The Task Group's layered air defence with SHARs, SKW helicopters, Sea Dart and Vulcan Phalanx proved reassuringly effective, even against such high quality opposition. The defences succeeded in inflicting significant attrition even against considerable numerical odds. It was assessed that only exercise rules had prevented the SHAR/SKW combination achieving even better results, especially in the early detection and destruction of shadowing aircraft. On the 24th ARK exercised her own offensive potential when the SHARs dropped 22 1,000 lb bombs on smoke flare targets.

The Task Group passed through the Suez Canal on 2 December and ARK berthed at Gibraltar a week later prior to the last lap home. On 13 December 801's SHARs disembarked in the Bay of Biscay. The same day HMS ILLUSTRIOUS met ARK and the two ships carried out a "two CVSG ASW PASSEX" as they proceeded northwards. On the 14th ARK anchored in Mounts Bay and disembarked her helicopters to Culdrose and Yeovilton. The final landmark of the cruise was a meeting between all three CVSGs, the first such occasion, south of Start Point. As the three ships steamed in close company the event was duly recorded in a memorable "PHOTEX". By evening ARK was at anchor at Spithead. After a final clean-up, and with more press embarked, ARK ROYAL finally came home on 15 December 1988, berthing at the South Railway Jetty. Families were soon reunited after six months' separation. The whole deployment had been a great success. Captain Harris reported that Outback had been "a happy though busy time which undoubtedly provided all concerned with a rich, varied and rewarding experience". The Ship's Company had been honed into an even more professional and tightly-knit team than normal. Rarely had a period of Christmas leave been better earned.

ARK ROYAL returned home to a more normal programme of NATO exercises. These marked the end of an era for, in 1989, the Berlin Wall came down and the Cold War confrontation that had conditioned the very existence of the ship and its primary anti-submarine task ended. This was still an unexpected and unlikely event when ARK ROYAL began conversion to her secondary LPH role for Exercise Cold Winter off Norway. Since the late 1960s the Royal Marines had emphasised their role as reinforcements to NATO's Northern Flank. At that time there were two dedicated LPHs, but these ships had become primarily CVSs before being sold or scrapped, the last to go being HERMES to India in the mid-1980s. It seemed natural, therefore, to continue to press the CVSGs into service periodically in this role. ARK was providing the helicopter spots to supplement those on the LPD Intrepid.

Fourteen Sea King 4 Commando helicopters (SKAs) of 845 and 846 Squadrons were embarked (most after the ship reached Norway) and were maintained on the after section of the hangar. The forward part of this space became a crowded mess deck for the embarked force of almost 400 extra personnel from 42 and 45 Commandos and 29 Battery Royal Artillery. There was also a detachment of Dutch marines. The weather was remarkably mild for the latitudes and time of year and created no problems. The highlight of the exercise was a 12-aircraft assault near Tromso. The ship then returned south bringing home 45 Commando, which disembarked by helicopter off Arbroath on 16 March. The SKAs disembarked to Yeovilton the following day, when ARK ROYAL returned to Portsmouth.

In a break between routine exercises on 27 April, while back at Portsmouth, Captain Harris handed over command to Captain John Brigstocke, one of the last traditional 'gunners' in the Navy, having come top in the last Long Course at HMS EXCELLENT at Whale Island. Captain Brigstocke's dynamism and force of character helped carry the ship through an extremely busy period that included exercises with Spanish Navy AV8B Matadors of the 9th Escuadrilla.

The ship berthed at Portsmouth on 7 July for a well-earned summer leave and self-maintenance period in which the port gearbox that had shed a tooth was repaired as part of a considerable programme of maintenance and defect rectification. After starring together with INVINCIBLE at Portsmouth Navy Days, the ship then sailed as the flagship of the new FOF2 Rear Admiral Peter Abbot to take part in Exercise Sharp Spear, the largest NATO maritime exercise of the year.

ARK ROYAL with FRS1 and SKW circa 1989.

Sharp Spear was a major exercise of the Shallow Seas campaign in NATO's CONMAROPS, ie operations in the Baltic, Baltic Approaches, North Sea and the waters surrounding the British Isles. ARK's contribution was the maintenance of sea control in the Western Approaches and she operated with Spanish and Dutch task groups, the former led by PRINCIPE DE ASTURIAS. The Spanish Matadors and 801 joined in an attack on the hulk of the old frigate HMS LEANDER which was finished off by 801 with three direct bomb hits and three close misses. As the ships passed around the north of Scotland and into the North Sea, attacks on ARK's group were carried out by a range of aircraft, American B52s and F16s, RAF Tornados, Buccaneers and Jaguars, Dutch, Belgian, Danish and Norwegian F6s, and Danish Drakens. 801 had great success splashing up to 14 aircraft in each sortie with the exercise luxury of in-flight weapon reloads!

The cancellation of Exercise Autumn Train relieved a too crowded programme and the ship could therefore begin a long assisted maintenance period at Portsmouth in October. Two diesel generators amid two auxiliary boilers were replaced and modifications made to the aircraft lifts. A large package of painting and preservation was also undertaken, as was work on the ship's undersides. YARD LTD contributed a free underwater survey. The work ensured a high level of material state and availability in subsequent trials. The ship was refitted to operate the latest Mk6 version of the Sea King ASW helicopter with which 820 was gradually re-equipping. During this period alongside, on 16 November, the Ship's Company exercised its right to march through the city of Leeds with bayonets fixed, drums beating and colours flying.

The first quarter of 1990 was taken up by work-up and sea training as well as preparations for an extended deployment to the Western Atlantic, Westlant 90, leading Task Unit 318.5.1 composed of ARK ROYAL, the frigates CUMBERLAND and BRAVE, the destroyer GLASGOW and the RFAs OLNA and FORT GRANGE. Things began on 18 April when ARK plus the two frigates sailed for exercise Jolly Roger, which would give useful anti-submarine practice with 'live' targets; 820 used the opportunity to gain experience of the tactical potential of its new aircraft, with their ability to operate eight sonobuoys.

On 1 May the three ships exercised with the American SSN PROVIDENCE while OLNA joined up and a major PASSEX began with French Task Force 471 led by the carrier FOCH. The two air groups each provided the threat. The very tight limits of pitch for operations by the French carrier prevented the full plans being effected but Sea Harriers and helicopters cross decked and invitations to lunch were exchanged. In all, the old Entente Cordiale was reasserted in no uncertain manner.

BRAVE joined the unit on 6 May and GLASGOW two days later. The following day the ships entered New York harbour for a successful five-day visit. ARK then left on the 13th with her air group lined up on deck and turned south for a visit and self-maintenance period, utilising the US Navy facilities at Mayport, Florida. During ARK's stay, which lasted for the rest of the month, relations with the Americans were maintained and strengthened through official and private functions, sport and official and squadron visits. Many officers and men took the opportunity to reunite with families flown over for the occasion. It was with rather heavy hearts among her Ship's Company that ARK sailed on 30 May to concentrate with the rest of the Task Group for Exercise Marcot.

Marcot was an exercise with the Royal Canadian Navy, whose assets formed a key component of the NATO Striking Fleet. The ships operated under the command of the Canadian Task Force 301, based in Bermuda, and the 5th Destroyer Squadron, led by the RCN helicopter-carrying destroyer ATHABASKAN. The lack of a submarine target limited ASW training opportunities but aircraft based in Bermuda provided excellent AAW training for the SHARs and SKWs. These aircraft also honed their skills as an anti-surface unit team. The exercise continued as the force moved northwards from Bermuda to Halifax, which was reached in thick fog on 15 June. The Task unit acquired a good understanding of both the strengths and weaknesses (especially in the AAW area) of the RCN.

ARK ROYAL arrived home at Portsmouth on 4 July for her Base Assisted Maintenance Period (BAMP) and Summer Leave Period. This marked a most significant stage in the ship's career as it saw the completion of Phase 1 of the conversion of the ship to carry female personnel with necessary modifications to two deck starboard. Accommodation was increased for both officers and junior rates, the ship's waste disposal system was improved, a large area of the flight deck represerved and the troublesome auxiliary boilers repaired in a most successful BAMP. The ship's ADAWS software was also updated.

On 3 September the ship sailed to act as FOF3s flagship for Teamwork 90. The Teamwork exercises were major demonstrations of NATO's ability to conduct maritime operations afloat and ashore in the key Norwegian Sea campaign of NATO's CONMAROPS. They had acquired particular importance with the emphasis on forward operations in the 1980s. However, by 1990, the exercise had been rather overtaken by events. Not only had relations with the Soviet Union been transformed but, more importantly, a new threat had appeared in the shape of Saddam Hussein who had invaded Kuwait. All American assets bound for Teamwork were diverted to Operation Desert Shield, the build-up in the Middle East to safeguard Saudi Arabia and put pressure on Saddam Hussein to withdraw. Teamwork thus went ahead with reduced forces and a revised programme between 6 and 17 September. There was an increased emphasis on the role of the British CVSGs and both INVINCIBLE and ARK ROYAL took part. ARK was the flagship of FOF3's ASW Striking Force covering the movement of an amphibious force to carry out landings at Namsos in northern Norway.

Britain had codenamed its contribution to the Gulf crisis Operation Granby and ARK ROYAL was nominated as contingency CVSG to be kept at 30 days' notice for deployment. On 15 October it looked as if she might be off to the Middle East as she sailed from Portsmouth and embarked her CAG 801 squadron, at full strength in pilots for the first time since the Falklands War and operating eight SHARs: 820 was still minus the two exercise casualties and 849B was minus one aircraft also. As the ship sailed for Gibraltar, 801 worked up its new pilots and 820 exercised surface search, fighter evasion and assault operations. A new era in the ship's operational role was beginning and change was symbolised by the departure of Captain Brigstocke at Gibraltar on the 23rd. He was replaced by Captain Neil E Rankin but would soon be back in the ship as Rear Admiral and Flag Officer Second Flotilla in command of Task Group 323.2, an important British contribution to the Gulf War of 1991.

In the event the Government decided that a CVSG was not immediately required. Instead the ship sailed for home on the 25 October, carrying out self-noise trials at Portland before arriving at Portsmouth on 1 November. There followed a period of uncertainty and contingency planning, largely spent alongside in the ship's home port. A debate was in progress over whether a CVSG was an appropriate augmentation of Britain's Gulf forces. While keeping herself in readiness for deployment in some form or other, the ship was available for work close to home and on 7 November she embarked two 820 SKJs and sailed for the South Western Approaches where two prototype Sea Harriers of the new and advanced FRS2 version from Boscombe Down carried out sea trials from the ship: 801 also exercised with the ship as part of its Granby preparations.

The waiting game at Portsmouth began once more on 16 November and continued over Christmas. In early January plans for JMC 911 were suddenly cancelled six days prior to the start of the exercise. With a military offensive about to take place to dislodge Saddam Hussein from his ill-gotten gains, the Government had belatedly made its mind up to send a carrier to the area. On 10 January ARK ROYAL left Portsmouth on Granby deployment as flagship of Task Group 232.2 with the frigate SHEFFIELD and the RFAs OLMEDA and REGENT in support. The following day ARK embarked her own air group that had been modified into a Granby configuration that reflected the expected operational profile of the ship. The eight Sea Harriers of 801 were supplemented by four normal SKJs of 820 and six more stripped of sonar for use in the utility role (coded SKU). One or two of the latter usually flew from OLMEDA. The ASW helicopters provided cover from a possible submarine threat, notably from Libya while the SKUs could be used for boarding operations in support of sanctions. Three SKWs of 849B provided radar cover. On the 13th ARK rendezvoused with the destroyers EXETER and MANCHESTER for successful Sea Dart firings, part of an intensive weapons training and work-up programme organised by the embarked FOF1 and FOF3 work-up staffs. MANCHESTER joined up with the Task Group and continued south with the other ships. Fast roping drills for boarding parties were conceived and practised, using the RFAs as targets after initial trials in ARK itself. The ship also familiarised itself with an enhanced communications fit.

Off Gibraltar, Rear Admiral Brigstocke (FOF2) arrived to use his former command as flagship of the Task group. The work-up staff of Flag Officer Naval Aviation also arrived to assist in training up the air group as the ship transited the Mediterranean. On 17 December as Desert Shield became Desert Storm and the Gulf War began in earnest, ARK ROYAL went to defence watches and the SHARs were armed each with four AIM-9L Sidewinder missiles and put on alert. Given both the unpredictability of Libya's ruler and the uncertainty of his support for Saddam Hussein, flying was curtailed on the 18th as the Task Group sailed by Libya.

On 22 January ARK ROYAL arrived off Cyprus. In the event she would go no further as there seemed to be opposition in London to ARK playing a more forward role. Reportedly the US Navy would have liked her to come at least into the Red Sea to lead the continued sanctions operations and to release American assets for more offensive deployment. But it was not to be. Only MANCHESTER went onward through the Suez Canal. Admiral Brigstocke and his group took up the important but rather frustrating role of surveillance of the vital Mediterranean sea lines of communication upon which the coalition forces in the Gulf depended. ARK ROYAL and her aircraft undertook the major share of the surveillance task and the maintenance of a comprehensive surface picture in the area. The ship also acted as AAW controller of the Eastern Mediterranean Sector of the Sixth Fleet's AAW control organisation, one of three such co-ordinated controllers covering the entire sea. As NATO's COMNAVSOUTH and

COMAIRSOUTH created a proper surveillance organisation the Task Group fused its efforts in a comprehensive picture compilation effort. ARK ROYAL acted as Force Over The Horizon Tactical Co-ordinator (FOTC) compiling and fusing the surface picture which was then transmitted on a Mediterranean-wide broadcast via JOTS.

There was an important role at first for 849B in providing daylight AEW cover for the force, flying up to five sorties a day, but the presence of NATO airborne early warning E3As allowed the pressure on the squadron to be diminished after 29 January. After that the SKWs flew AEW missions only at dawn and dusk and were able to be used more in the surface surveillance and targeting roles: 801 mainly concentrated on CAP against the possibility of Iraqi attack with an intensive flying programme at times. For two periods of 36 hours each, the squadron achieved two over two SHARs on CAP by day and one over one by night: 820 was kept busy with HDS and replenishment tasks (VERTREP) as well as surface search and probe missions.

A weekly VERTREP was maintained with RAF Akrotiri for fresh provisions and incoming stores. RAF Phantoms from Cyprus were frequent visitors for air defence exercises. The closest touch was kept with the Americans with a direct FLTSATCOM secure satellite link established with the flagship of the Sixth Fleet, the cruiser USS BELKNAP. This was backed up by a portable SATCOM terminal specially obtained from the US Navy at Rota complete with USN Chief Petty Officer to instruct ARK's communicators in its workings. The group operated with three US warships, the destroyer SPRUANCE and Aegis cruiser PHILIPPINE SEA together with the nuclear powered cruiser VIRGINIA that was an active participant in the Desert Storm strategic air campaign with her Tomahawk cruise missiles.

On 7 February the frigate HMS CHARYBDIS arrived to replace MANCHESTER and the opportunity was taken to carry out an ASuW exercise. The following day a ceasefire was announced but it was not until the 19th that the situation was assessed as stable enough for ARK ROYAL to revert to 30 minutes' notice for action. On the 24th the situation allowed TG 323.2 to depart the Cyprus area for Naples. Leaving the Cyprus rules of engagement area allowed the ship to revert to cruising watches. On 25 February the Task group exercised with the German Task group 501 of four DD/FF and two support ships that had been sent to the Mediterranean to relieve other assets sent to the Gulf: 801's SHARs carried out a most encouraging undetected exercise Sea Eagle attack on the German ships. As the German ships kept company, a Greek submarine provided a target for 820's rather under used SKJs.

ARK arrived in Naples on 1 March and Admiral Brigstocke delegated conduct of the Task Group to Captain Rankin under the Operational control of CINCFLEET: he hauled down his flag in ARK two days later. ARK sailed with RFA REGENT from Naples on March and the Task Group reformed briefly on 8 March. COMNAVSOUTH AND COMAIRSOUTH lowered the surveillance level and the Sixth Fleet disbanded the AAW control system shortly after; the impressive Mediterranean-wide air and sea surveillance picture faded away and ARK could find nothing on the frequencies that had once been so busy.

There was no doubt that the preceding weeks had seen an impressive demonstration of NATO's ability to conduct integrated maritime operations in the Mediterranean. To provide relaxation after the tensions of long hours at advanced states of readiness, ARK ROYAL visited Piraeus from 15 to 20 March and Palma from 27 March to 3 April. CHARYBDIS had already gone to NAVOCFORMED on the 11th but the rest of the group rendezvoused south of Ibiza on 4 April for a four-ship RAS. It transited the straits of Gibraltar the following day and finally she formally reverted to organic surveillance and linking procedures. Four days *later TG 323.2 began to dissolve as SHEFFIELD and REGENT detached to Devonport and OLMEDA to Portland. The SHARs also flew off to Yeovilton. Granby was finally over.

With the USSR in dissolution, and the Gulf situation absorbing US carriers, the exercise did not have a forward operations component. Instead of leading the Striking Fleet through the GRIUK gaps into the Norwegian Sea, ARK's group conducted ASW precursor operations in the South Western Approaches before transiting south to commence convoy escort operations in the Bay of Biscay. The carrier remained detached from the rest of the group in EMCON silence. She received the tactical picture by link from the escorts giving cover both to them and the convoy with her air group. The exercise was a 'freeplay' evolution and the carrier completely escaped submarine attack by this tactic. There were only a few air attacks that the SHAR/SKW combination proved effective in handling. The main problems for 801 were doubts about the reaction control system of the aircraft, which limited operations and eventually led to engine removal from all aircraft the following month. The ship also suffered her own difficulties with the catastrophic failure of the port outer Olympus.

The exercise terminated on 18 June and was followed by first a maintenance period on completing the conversion to carry female personnel and then another Westlant deployment. Many visitors were hosted on board and a visiting Omani delegation given dinner. Just over a week later on 10 September the ship was at sea once more sailing back across the Atlantic. One of the main objectives was Trial Woking, the development of SKJ Mk6 tactics on the AUTEC range at Andros Island. Beginning on 1 October, 250 hours were flown by the SKJs with 143 hours on contact time and nine Stingray torpedo drops.

On the way home via Gibraltar, a Chinook embarked with a Boscombe Down trials team to explore its operating limits from a CVSG flight deck. The trials necessitated finding rougher weather on the South Western Approaches rather than tarrying too long in the Gibraltar exercise areas and a demanding schedule was achieved with 80 hours of flying in nine days involving 400 deck landings.

Back home in Portsmouth, on 25 November ARK ROYAL received her first draft of 73 WRNS. They found the ship deep in a major enhanced DAMP that had begun on the 19th. The ship was about to enter dry dock and was depending on floating domestic arrangements moored close by. Nevertheless the women settled in remarkably well.

ARK was docked from 28 November to 4 February. A much-needed reverse osmosis water-making plant was installed to increase the water-making capacity of the ship to cope with the increases in the ship's complement over the original design capacity. The Oasis 4 data handling system with 70 terminals was also installed to improve stores service but the system was not without its teething troubles. The enormous amount of work required in the whole maintenance period could not have been carried out if the weather had not been unseasonably mild. The ship sailed for post DAMP trials on 12 February, the only serious problem being overheating in new bearings in the gearboxes.

ARK ROYAL trials the Sea Harrier FA2.

The WRNS were not the only new personnel on board. In fact, almost a third of the Ship's Company was new to the ship since the start of DAMP. The new crew needed working up to full efficiency and Captain Rankin and his officers instigated an intensive training programme.

A period of sea training saw confidence grow among ARK's men and women and Ship's Company morale improved noticeably. This was despite a very serious accident that took place on 20 April, Easter Monday. The SHARs were lobbing 28 lb practice bombs at a splash target astern. Due to a software failure, the correct 'aim off' was not applied to one bomb that landed on the flight deck, detonating as it penetrated into 2J2 messdeck where it injured five people.

Captain Rankin had every reason to be proud of his Ship's Company and the way they coped with the incident. Flag Officer Sea Training complimented the ship on its reaction: "the response teams, already sharpened up, acted with impressive speed and efficiency, preventing further tragedy." RNH Haslar described the initial treatment of the casualties as "exemplary".

In June ARK ROYAL began a tour around the UK in Exercise Shop Window. This was an attempt to sell the Navy to the widest and most influential audience possible and to explain that even with the end of the Gulf War it was as useful as ever in a wider range of roles in an unstable world. Captain Rankin was pleased to be able "to reach a lot of people who would otherwise not get the opportunity to meet the Navy, who live too far away from Navy Days ports". Then it was back to Portsmouth for a short period alongside before embarking Commander UK Task Group (as FOF2-Rear Admiral Brigstocke had now formally become) for Exercise Purple Monarch.

Over the weekend of 27-28 June, a Joint Force Operations Staff embarked in the ship. The ship left for Gibraltar on 29 June for the passage to Gibraltar exercising the Joint Force Headquarters (Afloat) under COMUKTG. The absence of her air group eased accommodation difficulties and the 20 per cent of her crew who were given leave resolved the problem completely. Delays were caused by foggy weather but all the passage and exercise procedures ran smoothly before the Staff were transferred to the LPD, HMS FEARLESS or ashore to Gibraltar to continue the exercise. Four RAF Chinook helicopters were carried on the flight deck, which were flown ashore as part of the exercise.

It was a new Captain who returned the ship to Portsmouth on 12 July 1992. Captain J J Blackham was fresh from Commodore posts as Director of the Royal Naval Staff College and Director of Naval Plans. As an intellectual officer with a degree in philosophy from the Open University, what better command opportunity could there be before promotion to Flag Rank? Carrier deployments to Westlant to take advantage of the US Navy's exercise facilities had been a regular feature of ARK's life and what turned out to be the last of the series began in September 1992. She was flagship of Task Group 610.01 flying the pennant of Flag Officer Surface Flotilla, Vice Admiral Sir Nicholas Hill-Norton. Exercises were held with the US Navy and visits made to Norfolk and Mayport which had become almost a home from home for ARK in recent years.

On the 13th ARK sailed from Mayport for exercises on the AUTEC range. The usual intense ASW activity took place with 820 in the forefront of activities, despite being reduced to only four operational airframes. Nevertheless, 140 hours of flying were achieved and successful use of the 2069 dipping sonar allowed a large number of attacks.

After a visit to Nassau, ARK sped back across the Atlantic for a major event planned for two years but scheduled to take place less than a week after the ship's arrival at Portsmouth. This was a dinner held by the Admiralty Board for Her Majesty the Queen to mark the 40th anniversary of her accession to the throne. Her Majesty and other members of the Royal Family were hosted at a dinner in the hangar by a most distinguished company of Officers headed by Admiral Sir Julian Oswald, the First Sea Lord. Every available Commanding Officer of Her Majesty's Ships was there. In many ways this was the culmination of the ship's career as a showpiece and flagship during her first period of service. More serious events were in the offing.

The ship then underwent her usual Base Assisted Maintenance period during which ARK's programme, which included both a JMC and an amphibious exercise, was transformed by the decision to send a naval task group to the Adriatic to support Operation Grapple, the deployment of British troops ashore as part of the United Nations Protections Force maintaining humanitarian aid during the Bosnian civil war that had followed the break up of Yugoslavia. The situation ashore was deteriorating and deployment of a contingency naval force was imperative. The last, and perhaps most important, stage of ARK's brief life so far was about to begin.

3
'GRAPPLE' AND 'HAMDEN'
ARK ROYAL IN THE ADRIATIC 1993-94

ARK ROYAL began to prepare for deployment on 8 January 1993. The situation was that the forces ashore in Bosnia on peacekeeping and humanitarian aid duties might have to be supported with heavier firepower or even evacuated under fire. This required a secure national base and a source of air support, both fixed and rotary winged, untrammelled by local sensitivities; a classic setting for an aircraft carrier.

The flexibility of a ship like ARK ROYAL was demonstrated by the reconfigured CAG, eight SHARs (two extra aircraft from 800 Squadron), three SKWs and eight Sea King 4 Commando helicopters of 846 Squadron to provide the support helicopter lift required to land reinforcements ashore and/or get the troops out. 820 Squadron was farmed out to two RFAs, four in FORT GRANGE and two in OLWEN. The Commando helicopters required the acquisition of large amounts of new equipment and a 'Fly Away Pack' in a four-tonne truck and trailer was provided. Stores holdings were generally improved and the ship fitted, as she had been in Purple Monarch, with an enhanced command and control suite so that she could act as a Joint Force HQ if required.

The ship sailed for a short shakedown and work-up on 14 January and the air group joined the following day. She was part of Task Force 612, operationally controlled by CINCFLEET under the command of CINC UK Land Forces. The CVSG Task Group, designated TG 612.02, was commanded by Captain Blackham. In addition to ARK ROYAL, it sailed with the frigates COVENTRY and BRILLIANT, RFA OLWEN and the aviation training ship RFA ARGUS. She was acting as an interim LPH with six 105 mm light guns from 29 Commando Regiment Royal Artillery, two batteries and HQ elements of 94 Locating Regiment RA and the Mortar Locating Troop of 29 Cdo Regiment RA. ARK's SKAs could deliver all but the heaviest vehicles. ARGUS was carrying 176 vehicles and trailers and 329 military personnel. FORT GRANGE joined the group on the 17th.

Captain Blackham's orders were to poise his CVSG Task Group in the Adriatic within five hours of Split by 26 January, being prepared to land reinforcements from ARGUS in support of British forces ashore. The group might have to participate in a withdrawal, enforce the No Fly Zone over the country, or provide air support to troops ashore. ARK could also operate as an offshore Joint Force HQ if required. As ARK ROYAL transited the South Western Approaches, the CAG worked up to combat efficiency with 801 exercising its air combat skills against Tornados, Buccaneers, Hunters, Falcons and Canberras, as well as the use of radar ranging for dive bombing attacks with 1,000 lb bombs. 846 used the SHARs to exercise helicopter evasion tactics and, once the Gibraltar exercise areas were reached, the landing of the forces embarked in ARGUS. Two SHARs had to be sent back to Yeovilton because of mechanical problems. One was swapped for another and the other returned after repairs.

After a brief pause at Gibraltar, the TG moved eastwards on the 23rd. It eventually entered the Adriatic on the 27th and Captain Blackham immediately conferred with the commanders of the ground forces in the Flagship. Its role was to be de-escalatory with no aggressive acts, as it remained 'poised' awaiting developments ashore. It is one of the great assets of sea power that it can thus provide decision makers with on the spot options, without the dangers of over commitment or entanglement. This was of special importance in such a confused situation as Bosnia, with everyone fighting everyone else.

ARK ROYAL and its CAG exercised the various actions it might be called upon to carry out. An airhead was established at Bari with a weekly dedicated Hercules flight from the United Kingdom and a large amount of HDS activity. Some changes occurred to the force as COVENTRY departed for her Armilla commitment on 9 February being replaced by her sister ship BRAZEN.

Soon after ARK arrived, the USA and France deployed carrier task groups in the area based around JOHN F KENNEDY and CLEMENCEAU respectively, and a US Marine Amphibious Force was also present. Two complementary blockade operations were in progress in the Southern Adriatic and Straits of Otranto. Captain Blackham made it his business to create the closest possible co-operation between forces present while maintaining the national character of his group. The Americans hosted a meeting on the JFK that agreed a programme of cross training and visits. 801 took advantage of this for air combat training with both American and French aircraft and simulated Sea Eagle strikes on both groups.

On 14 February the likelihood of imminent intervention seemed less and the Group was stood down to 24 hours notice off Split. The two extra SHARs were returned to the UK. On the 26th ARK ROYAL entered Trieste for a well earned run ashore and recuperation period after six weeks continuously at sea.

In March the routine of poise and training was started once more. 801 disembarked with five aircraft to hone their bombing skills at RAF Decimomannu and the Capo Frasca range in Sardinia. The aim was to gradually increase bomb release height so that the 1,000 lb bombs could be delivered outside the range of small arms fire and hand held SAMs. An encounter exercise was held with the Italian frigate ZEFFIRO in which 849B's SKWs co-operated with RFA-based 820 SKJs in surveillance and probe tactics.

March saw a welcome visit to Piraeus and BRILLIANT departed to be relieved by the Dutch frigate ABRAHAM CRIJNSSEN. Rules of engagement and exchange of information problems were solved in another demonstration of the ease with which friendly navies can co-operate together, at least in relatively low threat environments. On the 11th, 279 personnel were flown home from ARGUS to be kept at 48 hours notice; this relieved pressure on a ship never designed to carry so many people. Eight days later the ship disembarked four SK4s to FORT AUSTIN and the passage home. March also saw visits by the Prince of Wales and FOSF and the roulement of the American battle group with the arrival of the USS THEODORE ROOSEVELT.

BRAZEN was replaced by BROADSWORD at the beginning of April. All seemed quiet in early April as 801 went back to exercising AAW skills while maintaining expertise in bombing by trials against splash targets. These culminated in the dropping from medium altitude of 14 inert 1,000 lb bombs with satisfying accuracy using steep dive deliveries.

The situation was quiet enough for a long visit to Naples for self-maintenance, beginning on the 13th and lasting nine days. The landmark event of this visit was a change of command on 21 April as Captain Blackham returned to promotion and the job of Chief of Staff to CINCNAVHOME. The new Commanding Officer was Captain Terry Loughran, an experienced aviator and MOD warrior with exactly the right instincts for the challenges the ship would soon have to face. He sailed with his Group on the 22nd and on the following day, increased tension ashore – the interposition of a Canadian unit between warring factions at Srebrenica – caused TG 612.02 to be reduced to 24 hours notice. 801's capacity to give close air support if needed was greatly improved on 26 April as the ship re-entered the Adriatic. The SHARs were officially declared capable of delivering Paveway 2 laser guided bombs; trials had been held by 801 personnel at Garvie Range in the UK and seven out of seven hits were obtained. On the 29th a Carrier Borne Ground Liaison Officer was embarked. Exercises were flown with aircraft from the THEODORE ROOSEVELT to prove both laser designation technique and laser designation options.

On 26 April another important event occurred. The Security Council in New York passed Resolution 820 calling for

Task group 612.02 in the Adriatic, ARK ROYAL with Fort Grange, Orangeleaf and Brave.

a much more stringent blockade of Serbia and Montenegro. This was being enforced by NATO's Standing Naval Force Mediterranean (TF432) off Montenegro and a Western European Union Force in the Strait of Otranto (TG621.1). The Yugoslav Navy began to respond to the tighter sanctions by adopting a more threatening posture and SNFM's commander Rear Admiral Martinotti asked both for surface combat air patrol (SUCAP) and more ships. BROADSWORD, with her two helicopter flight, was cleared to be tasked to give the necessary cover with her Sea Skua equipped Lynx and on 17 May TG 610.02 was authorised to support TF 432 under its rules of engagement with air or surface support as required.

A third element in this jigsaw puzzle was Exercise Deny Flight ordered on 12 April following Security Council

Resolution 818. This attempt to stop flying by the participants in the Bosnian War was being co-ordinated by NATO's Fifth Tactical Air Force HQ in Vincenza. The imposition of the air limitations had effects on carrier operations and a liaison team was sent to Vincenza on 3 May to work out arrangements for the integration of ARK's flying into the overall developing scheme.

On 4 May, the frigate DE RUYTER replaced CRIJNSSEN and shortly afterwards ORANGELEAF joined the TG to replace OLWEN which was away on self-maintenance in Crete; she detached again on the 22nd. ARGUS also detached on the 10th for an SMP at Trieste. ARK ROYAL was being supported by regular flights to and from an airhead at Bari and on the 18th hosted local dignitaries on board while at sea. That day was notable in a more important sense as it saw Rear Admiral Brigstocke assume command of the Task Group. It had been a political decision not to send the Commander of the UK Task Group to lead TG 612 in person. In May however, with tensions increasing and a risk of air strikes, CINCFLEET thought it desirable that COMUKTG take personal command for a temporary period. The admiral arrived in his familiar flagship on the 19th and began a strenuous programme of visits to familiarise himself with the situation.

On 24 May ARK arrived at Corfu for a four-day visit during which Captain Loughran laid a wreath at the grave of the 44 sailors killed in the incident in the nearby Channel in 1946. During that time her notice was revised to allow her to visit Malta for self-maintenance. Another period on station came first, as she had to return to the Adriatic to resume her SUCAP duties. On the 4th May ARGUS finally put into Split to offload some of her vehicles before sailing for home the following day.

ARK arrived in Malta for her SMP on 8 June. This was the first time a British carrier had been in Grand Harbour since the previous ARK ROYAL had visited in 1978. An estimated 30,000 people, a tenth of the island's population, turned out to visit the ship which received a rousing welcome and send-off. It was all a wonderful demonstration of the undying affection of the old naval base island for the Royal Navy.

By the time ARK returned to the Adriatic, the two separate blockade operations, Maritime Guard by NATO and Sharp Fence by WEU, had been united on 15 June into a single operation. Sharp Guard had an integrated Task Force 440 with three Task Group Commands, two provided by NATO's standing forces and one by the WEU's former CTF432. The ship was back on station on 18 June and the following day the Admiral lunched with Rear Admiral Martinotti, CTG 440.1 and Admiral Johnson of the American TF60, Admiral Brigstocke was rightly anxious to obtain the greatest level of co-ordination possible between these forces.

On 20 and 26 June, the SHARs were once more on alert to support Admiral Martinotti's ships. There were three Alert 30 aircraft, two carrying a single 1,000 lb bomb and two 30 mm cannon and the third carried two Sea Eagle missiles. On these occasions there were usually two exercise launches per day. In between, on the 22nd, a flight of 820 Squadron returned home to ARK ROYAL from OLWEN with its two SKJs. On 28 June the ship sailed south to meet the Italian aircraft carrier GARIBALDI for training and cross decking and a VIP visit by the Italian defence minister and senior naval officers.

The passing of Security Council Resolution 836 with the possibility of close air support for UNPROFOR, especially those allocated to designated protected areas, led the Chief of the Defence Staff to offer on 7 July ARK ROYAL's SHARs to

NATO's Supreme Allied Commander Europe to help carry out the strikes should they prove necessary. Contingency planning for this involvement, code named Discipline Guard, continued apace and 801 took part in Exercise Crater in Italy from 19-20 July to familiarise itself with procedures. On 23 July, there were two aircraft on board ARK at Alert 30 for close air support missions in Bosnia.

On 12 July, designated successor to Admiral Brigstocke, Rear Admiral Mike Gretton arrived on board and the change of command occurred on the 13th as the SHARs stood on yet another dawn to dusk session of SUCAP duty. The ship entered Palermo harbour for a last Mediterranean port visit and sailed on the 29th for the awaited hand over and

ARK ROYAL (left) handing over Bosnia patrol to Invincible. 2 February 1994.

Flag transfer to her sister ship INVINCIBLE. The last seven months had been a period of very hard work for ARK ROYAL, her CAG and her crew. As Captain Loughran put it: "Poise is about living at sea, striking the balance between keeping your military skills at a high level so that you can respond should you have to and yet not staying at such a high level that you become stale. We had to strike a balance between work and play and it is perhaps worth remembering that the work has consisted of 80 per cent of our time at sea and only 20 per cent of our time in harbour. Over 1,000 men and women sailed at very short notice in January with great uncertainty as to how long they would be away and what they would be doing. As the months have gone by and the task has become more clear one can only admire the motivation of those on board and the fortitude of the families at home who lent their unstinting support."

Back in Portsmouth, ARK ROYAL underwent her period of base assisted maintenance. She was back at sea in November for work-up with a reduced air group and then spent Christmas alongside. The government had been considering withdrawal of British forces in the Spring but had decided to stick it out for another year. The whole operation in former Yugoslavia had now been re-christened Operation Hamden with 'Grapple' reserved for the ground forces in Bosnia. This necessitated a change of programme for ARK. Only two CVSGs are normally kept in service at any one time. It had been planned that the ship would decommission in the summer for a period in reserve and a major refit. That was now to be delayed until the beginning of September. On Friday 28 January ARK ROYAL sailed for pre-deployment training en route to her operational station. She embarked an air group of eight SHARs from 801 Squadron, seven SKJs from

849 B flight helicopter.

820 and three SKW from 849B. The group exercised on the way to Gibraltar with 820 working the frigate Cumberland on her way in the same direction, but bound for Armilla. At the end of the month, ARK met her sister ILLUSTRIOUS, now out of refit and a future relief in the Hamden roster.

On 4 February, ARK ROYAL arrived at Gibraltar for a four-day visit. Here INVINCIBLE handed on the torch of Operation Hamden after an 'ENCOUNTEREX' in which each carrier attacked the other for exercise with Sea Eagle SHARs. Captain Loughran assumed command once again of Task Group 512.02, subordinate to the Hamden Joint Force Headquarters Wilton. 801 disembarked for bombing practice at Decimomanu. That weekend a mortar bomb at Sarajevo caused heavy loss of life which reinforced the calls for air strikes against the offending artillery.

On the 10th, ARK ROYAL received a NATO Fifth Allied Tactical Air Force request to be available as soon as possible to support operations over Bosnia Herzegovina. The planned port visit to Naples had already been cancelled. The ship was moving eastwards to re-embark 801 Squadron on 10 February, their range exercises having been successfully telescoped. On the 10th, the North Atlantic Council met to approve air strikes around Sarajevo, if requested by the UN Secretary General. The following day however, General Rose, the newly appointed British commander of UNPROFOR in Bosnia brokered a ceasefire deal in which Bosnian Serb artillery would withdraw from around the city. A deadline was set for compliance.

When the ship took up station on the 13th its SHARs were deployed on a contingency basis in case UNPROFOR found itself under attack by one of the factions and required close air support. Intensive air activity however, was also useful to pressurise the Bosnian Serbs into accepting the Rose Plan. The flights over Bosnia were part of the Deny Flight operations to prevent any side using air power in the Bosnian war. British SHARs were now an integral and important part of this operation. It had been proved that carrier-based fighters could fly when air stations ashore in Italy were fogged, thus maintaining a necessary fighter presence. The Sea Harriers were also capable of carrying out useful reconnaissance. On the first day of Deny Flight operations, four pairs of SHARs flew on close air support sorties and one pair on reconnaissance.

ARK ROYAL was one of three nationally controlled carrier groups in the area, the others being based around the French carrier FOCH and the American SARATOGA. All gave their governments a useful range of options. Their aircraft were also available to support Task Force 440 on blockade duty if it was threatened. That force included two British ships, CHATHAM and BIRMINGHAM.

As the deadline ran out the SHARs kept up an intensive flying programme of 'exercise close air support' (XCAS) and recce missions, sometimes as many as 14. Commander UK Task Group, Admiral Gretton, arrived on St Valentine's Day and decided to assume command in case events took an ugly turn. But by the 18th it was clear that the Serbs had begun withdrawal of heavy weapons and the very real threat of air strikes began to recede. Nevertheless, it was not until the 21 February that it became clear that ARK ROYAL would not have to attack its designated target in the air strike plan.

On 22 February, ARK's SHARs were called to support an attacked convoy but the situation was too confused for them to drop their 1,000 lb bombs. The following day, HMS COVENTRY, TG 612.02's accompanying frigate, sent a team on board ARK to discuss how best that ship's capabilities could be exploited by the group. Also on the 23rd a crucial peace agreement was signed in Zagreb between the Bosnian Croat forces, the HVO, and the predominantly Muslim Bosnian National Army. On the 24th, with tension reduced, Admiral Gretton returned to the UK. ARK stood down from Deny Flight operations the following day and came to anchor in the Gulf of Manfredonia.

This rest was cut short by the request from 5th ATAF for ARK to plug gaps in the Deny Flight programme caused by fog in Italy and the absence of the SARATOGA alongside in Trieste. The importance of these missions was emphasised on 28 February when USAF F16s engaged five Galeb aircraft flying on a bombing mission for the Bosnian Serbs. Four were destroyed and the fifth badly damaged. ARK's SHARs were next on call and might have been the aircraft involved. They were vectored onto a fleeting helicopter contact but it faded before it could be sighted.

One of the finest views of ARK ROYAL in the Adriatic in 1994 was taken as the ship rendezvoused with Sir Tristram carrying reinforcement vehicles for UNPROFOR (above and right). (*EJ Grove collection*)

Early March should have seen the ship in Toulon but instead she was at Bari, closer to her operational station with expected events ashore in mind. There she was joined for an overnight visit by Admiral Gretton, hosting the House of Commons Defence Committee which was clearly impressed with the ship's vital role. After demonstrating the ship's support for UNPROFOR to the Committee, it was a move south for weapon training in the Ionian Sea, before resuming Deny Flight. The air group was reduced by one SHAR being sent back to Yeovilton because of pressure on airframe numbers during the FRS2 programme. Maintaining the flying programme with only seven aircraft was not easy, especially as there were inevitable serviceability problems with the remaining airframes: at least one SHAR had to have a complete engine change. Two SKJs were also deployed on the RFA FORT AUSTIN, one of the two such ships providing vital underway support for the force (the other was RFA OLWEN). Usually therefore, ARK was on station with an air group of seven SHARs, five SKJs and three SKWs, not a lavish provision in the circumstances.

One of 801 Squadron's Sea Harriers on a Deny Flight mission over Bosnia. (EJ Grove collection)

The ship was soon back on station primarily to support vital humanitarian convoy activity that was in danger of being seriously opposed, but also more generally to assert a NATO air presence to persuade the locals of the power available should they push the United Nations too far. The ARK's presence was especially critical at this time as the French carrier group was being changed and the SARATOGA was absent on exercise in the Eastern Mediterranean. ARK's normal programme was to fly five pairs of SHARs, ie 10 sorties a day, eight XCAS and two reconnaissance. The recce aircraft were kept on alert for battle damage assessment should an attack be carried out but would go out in the afternoons to help improve the general picture of the evolving situation ashore. The SHARs' photo-recce capability had been little used before the operations in the Adriatic but was now really coming into its own.

On the XCAS missions, exercises were carried out with forward air controllers ashore to which SHARs were assigned by controllers in American EC-130H Hercules aircraft. As an alternative to the more normal programme, three-hour offensive counter air (OCA) missions were flown as part of the campaign to prevent breaches of the No Fly Zone. During these missions the SHARs had to refuel in flight from airborne RAF Tristar tankers. The efficiency of 801, ably led by the quiet, determined Lt Cdr Mel Robinson, impressed everyone they worked with. The aircraft, even on recce missions, carried a 1,000 lb bomb on the centreline and an AIM-9M Sidewinder missile under each wing, meaning that they were available to deal with threats on the ground and in the air. Because of the height at which the aircraft were normally operating (over 5,000 ft) cannon were not of much use and it was decided not to carry them. This lowered the weight of the aircraft, a critical factor in the warm air of the Adriatic. Every time Harriers were launched the ship had to work up to quite high speeds, with much vibration aboard in the after part of the ship.

820 was much in demand, largely in the transport role, although the existence of one or two operational Yugoslav submarines advised maintaining skills with the dipping sonar. 849B helped out with HDS and VIP taxi work; one of its helicopters was the first to establish HDS connection with Split. The squadron also carried out periodic surface surveillance and navigation training missions. The SKWs were often detached ashore to work both with the RAF and the Italian Navy who were interested in helicopter AEW for their carrier. The main operational AEW work was carried out by high flying E3s whose picture was transmitted to Adriatic ships via LINK 11. An American Aegis cruiser colourfully known as Red Crown and based in TF 440's area of operations to the south was the area air warfare co-ordinator. The SKWs presence was, however, reassuring especially if maverick elements tried surface attacks with fast attack craft.

If the conflict escalated ashore, such hostile action could not be ruled out, especially if carrier-based air power was involved. A close watch was kept on the Yugoslav and Croatian Navies and Falcon aircraft were flown out to simulate missiles to help ARK practice action in her own self defence. Exercises with them had been carried out in the Ionian Sea training period in March.

The fog of the Adriatic justified the carrier's presence on many occasions, but it was sometimes tricky finding clear areas of sea and manoeuvring in them at the speeds required to operate aircraft. Based on the weather forecast the ship would move, perhaps 80 miles overnight, to find the best operating area expected for the day. ARK operated unescorted, although at least one RFA was usually in the vicinity and RAS operations were regularly conducted to top up with both fuel and a wide range of solid stores. The latter replenishments usually took place once a fortnight. As well as jackstay transfers, the vertical replenishments (VERTREPS) were particularly impressive for observers to watch with their intricately choreographed helicopter movements and their conversion of the busy flight deck into an even busier place than usual.

Up to 120 tons of stores provisions and ammunition were transferred per RAS. Large numbers of personnel from all departments were involved, at the dumps where the heavy jackstays brought over the pallets, moving pallets across the deck and down into the hangar where they were broken down and finally taken down the internal lifts into the storerooms or magazines. The physical transfer between ships took about two hours, with up to 100 separate loads arriving by jackstay or helicopter. A further four hours were required to strike all the stores below.

There was some time for port visits in the Med.

Helicopters were also flown in and out of Split allowing members of the Ship's Company to go ashore to acquaint themselves with conditions there and for Army personnel to visit the ship. For both sides it was a welcome break even if it also involved playing a full part in a day's work both afloat and ashore.

In order to maintain efficiency some rest and recreation needed to be given to ARK's hard working Officers and Company, so the ship maintained its programme of port visits, as operational dynamics allowed. An 11-day visit to Piraeus, with families coming out for an all too brief period with their loved ones, was much appreciated and many took the opportunity to visit some of the nearby Greek islands. Weather throughout the stay was generally good apart from one day when the heavens opened and seemed to remain open all day with torrential downpours, which, in the event, proved fortuitous.

For six months the floating airfield that is ARK ROYAL and the complex community on board patrolled up and down the increasingly balmy waters of the Adriatic, constantly monitoring the weather to find the best flying conditions. Its aircraft continued to play a vital role supporting UNPROFOR in general and the enhanced BRITFOR in particular. Many of the Ship's Company were able to get ashore into Bosnia to spend time with either 845 Squadron or various British Army units and in return ARK was able to host a number of British Army personnel from ashore together with various visitors from French and American ships in the Adriatic.

It was very gratifying for the Ship's Company to hear from those who had been ashore in Bosnia how much UNPROFOR appreciated the ubiquitous SHARs overhead and the reassuring presence of Britain's Flagship somewhere over the horizon; ready to protect them when threatened and to get them out of harm's way if the situation deteriorated.

According to the soldiers, the SHARs seemed to possess a remarkable ability to pacify the belligerents whenever their engines were heard overhead. In one such incident among many, the SHARs arrived on the scene at the newly established BritBat 2 (Duke of Wellington's Regiment) HQ at Bugojno just as it was under bombardment from BSA artillery. Two British soldiers were wounded but the guns stopped at the sight and sound of the SHARs and before more casualties could be suffered. The very same day the Nordic Battalion called in a pair of ARK's SHARs to cover a successful convoy on the difficult Route Mario. Overnight, in a far from certain meteorological situation, ARK sped northwards to find the optimum weather to make sure her SHARs could be over Bugojno at dawn the following day to deter further action. Early the following morning the weather remained marginal, nevertheless the pair of SHARs was successfully launched and did its job effectively as always.

What was without doubt the most dramatic incident of the deployment was to follow in the wake of the ship's visit to Greece. On sailing from Piraeus on Monday 11 April, ARK ROYAL was requested to be on station in the Adriatic 24 hours earlier than expected to provide extra close air support in the wake of the BSA's offensive against Gorazde. US aircraft had by then carried out the first two live CAS missions over Bosnia. By the end of the week the situation had deteriorated and a large number of badly wounded Muslim civilians were in the process of being evacuated by the helicopters of 845 Squadron base in Split. On the afternoon of Saturday 15 April two SHARs being flown by Lt Nick Richardson and Lt 'Oz' Phillips were on patrol over the area when they were directed to the

Gorazde enclave where tanks were firing into the town. One of the tanks was also firing at a hospital full of wounded civilians and shells were landing in the close vicinity of UN forces. Both aircraft were 'Cleared Hot' to engage the tanks. However, in order to avoid collateral damage, it was necessary for the aircraft to fly three passes to clearly identify the target. On the first pass the wingman was engaged by a missile believed to be an SA7 heat seeker which narrowly missed his aircraft. Despite the danger to themselves the two aircraft pressed home their attack in response to the desperation of the situation conveyed by the UN troops on the ground.

A missile hit the first aircraft, being flown by Lt Nick Richardson, and he was forced to eject. He was subsequently picked up by the BiH and was taken to a UN Joint Command Cell in Gorazde where he remained for 36 hours. Within two days he was returned to the ship where he enjoyed a spirited reunion with his squadron. He was in good condition, apart from a few scratches and was airborne again within four days.

The pilots of both these aircraft displayed considerable courage and professionalism in their continued attempts to carry out their mission, despite having come so close to being killed on the first attempt. CNN gave an incomplete report of the action within 10 minutes, prompting Captain Loughran to speak to the press with the full story of the pilots' bravery. ARK was in the headlines again.

After an extended period of Deny Flight the ship left the Adriatic for a delayed and much deserved short break in Corfu where she met up with a number of other ships from the task group.

Upon leaving Corfu, ARK sailed towards Palma to team up with an armada of 93 warships from 10 NATO nations in order to take part in Exercise DYNAMIC IMPACT 94, the largest NATO maritime exercise of its kind since the end of the Cold War. The exercise was designed to test NATO's ability to protect her sea lines of communication in the Mediterranean and carry out a major amphibious operation. The exercise enabled ARK ROYAL to demonstrate the capability and flexibility of an aircraft carrier as a means of power projection.

The 10-day exercise ended with a visit to Palma where the ARK was able to conduct a much needed SMP and the Ship's Company were able to enjoy what was undoubtedly one of the most popular visits of the deployment. Throughout DYNAMIC IMPACT and the subsequent visit to Palma, the Command continued to monitor the situation in Bosnia so that ARK could return at a moment's notice if the situation demanded.

When the ARK eventually returned to the Adriatic at the beginning of June, Brigadier Ridgway, the new commander of BRITFOR in Bosnia was able to visit the ship and report a marked improvement in the situation ashore. The American-brokered ceasefire between Bosnian Croats and Muslims had held remarkably well, however it had given the Muslims easier access to arms supplies from Croatia. Only having to fight on one front, the Muslims were able to focus their efforts on the Serbs and a renewed onslaught pushed back the BSA in a number of areas. However, it appeared that the war was reaching its culminating point. Soldiers and civilians alike seemed to be weary of war; only some military and political leaders appeared to relish the prospect of continued fighting. The UN forces on the ground were taking advantage of this to try and normalise the situation ashore, re-opening schools, providing essential services and repairing the war-shattered infrastructure. A number of ARK personnel were able to get ashore and help with this vital work. In view of the gradually improving situation ashore it was clear that the same intense level of Deny Flight activity would not now be required. By 8 June there had been a breakthrough at the Geneva talks. All three sides signed a Cessation of Hostilities, which came into effect on 10 June.

Her job done, ARK handed over to INVINCIBLE and sailed for home. In September there was a visit to Newcastle, appropriately where both the ship and Captain Loughran were laid down! Then it was back to Portsmouth for an indeterminate period of 'Preservation by Operation' to be followed by a major refit. The first phase in the life of the ship was over, a period in which the fifth ARK ROYAL had added still further lustre to an already famous name. She had shown the flag, contributed to the end of the Cold War and then played a central role in establishing operations required to stabilise a disordered world. Her presence had provided Britain with leverage out of all proportion to the investment in her.

4 THE REFIT

After over four years in reserve at Portsmouth, HMS ARK ROYAL arrived at Rosyth Dockyard on 11 May 1999 to begin a two and a half-year transformation at the hands of Babcock Rosyth Defence Ltd (BRDL). The Royal Navy's flagship aircraft carrier made a striking sight as she slipped under the famous Forth Bridges in the Firth of Forth on the final leg of her six-day passage from Portsmouth.

Bereft of her engines and many systems, which had been removed during the lay-up period, ARK ROYAL was towed all the way into Rosyth Dockyard by two tugs to begin a special refit that would significantly extend her capabilities and life expectancy.

This refit was to see her flight deck extended and hangar upgraded to enable better operation of the RAF's GR7 Harrier aircraft and, for the first time from an aircraft carrier, the ability to fly and accommodate the Merlin anti-submarine warfare helicopter, as well as a major upgrade of systems.

ARK ROYAL's arrival also heralded a new chapter for the specialist ship refitting company, BRDL, which would deliver the refit to the Ministry of Defence. The company is widely experienced and highly expert at carrying out surface ship refits, having fulfilled this role for eight decades, and has first class docking and support facilities. ARK ROYAL made history by becoming the first aircraft carrier to come into Rosyth Dockyard for refit. BRDL, a trading arm of Dockyard owners Babcock Engineering Services Ltd, part of the Babcock International Group, was all geared up for the refit having already spent two years in the planning stages. The company even went to the lengths of buying a seven ft long, scale model of the ship and having some Dockyard apprentices build a scale model of No1 dock to check how the vessel would fit.

An early indication of the beneficial team work that was to develop during the refit period was the charity effort of five of the ship's crew and five BRDL employees who joined forces to cycle from Portsmouth to Rosyth, mirroring ARK ROYAL's journey to the Dockyard. The cyclists claim they won

ARK ROYAL arrives in the Firth of Forth under tow for her major refit in May 1999.
(Mike Tazioli, Babcock Engineering Services Ltd)

by arriving at Rosyth first, raising £10,000 in the process for charities. BRDL donated £5,000 to the Children's Hospice Association Scotland (CHAS) and, in recognition of ARK ROYAL being affiliated with the City of Leeds, the Ship's Company chose to split its £5,000 between a local school for blind people and a cancer charity based in Leeds.

ARK ROYAL had been laid up at Portsmouth on a care and maintenance basis for over four years where she was in a 'state of extended readiness' meaning, in theory, she could become operational within three months. Structurally she was in a fair condition and her flight deck had recently received a coat of paint. Key machinery and parts of her systems had been removed to be used on other vessels or to be returned to MoD stores. The equipment remaining on board had been preserved and her funnels and sea inlets had been covered. Her lay-up presented BRDL with a unique opportunity as well as some unusual problems. Planners and estimators were able to visit the ship on a number of occasions before she arrived at Rosyth. The drawback was that they did not actually see her operational.

Strategic planning began back in January 1997. Babcock has a close and successful working relationship with its MoD customer on site, the Warship Support Agency (Rosyth). On the ARK ROYAL refit, BRDL helped draw up the specification and costs for this massive task and formal meetings took place every two weeks. Probably the biggest difficulty facing the BRDL team was the logistics of carrying out a constantly growing refit package on a vessel this size.

ARK ROYAL makes a striking sight as she arrives in the Firth of Forth in May 1999.
(Mike Tazioli, Babcock Engineering Services Ltd)

The ship becomes a building site.
(Mike Tazioli, Babcock Engineering Services Ltd)

Throughout the contract period the customer presented variations to the contract, meaning the estimated 853,000 man-hours would double to 1.6 million, and all to be carried out in the original timescale. These challenges were met head-on thanks to BRDL's vast experience and expertise, planning down to the finest detail and the vital teamwork.

A combination of update work and many sizeable A&As (Alteration and Additions), that is, changes to the ship's structure, fabric and facilities, made up the refit package. One of the main tasks was to extend the flight deck to accommodate more easily the GR7 Harrier fixed wing aircraft and the Merlin anti-submarine warfare helicopter. Other major changes included removing one of the ship's main forms of defence, the Sea Dart anti-aircraft missile system, mainly to free up space for modifications to accommodate the aircraft and also because it was deemed surplus to requirements. A major system upgrade involving new communications equipment was also completed and messes, sleeping quarters and offices for the ship's staff were refurbished.

After her arrival at the South Arm of the Dockyard on 11 May 1999, ARK ROYAL moved into the Entrance Lock where she spent the night. The following day she was towed to J&K Berth and, three weeks later, on 15 June 1999, she was moved into No1 Dock. A week and a half later the water was drained and she was 'docked down' for structural surveys to begin. While in dry dock all her external steelwork was blasted back to bare steel and a holding primer applied while certain structural tasks were carried out. Holes were cut in the outer bottom to allow access to the ship's tanks – these carry diesel, aircraft fuel, fresh water and dirty oil – as well as to the watertight compartments and trim tanks. Surveying, blasting and any structural repairs were carried out before the massive, five-month job of renewing paint coatings began. As the ship will deploy and operate a greater number of aircraft she needed extra storage for aircraft fuel so some of the tanks containing dieso, which powers the diesel engines, were converted to carry the aviation fuel, avcat.

Within the mechanical part of the contract some 30,000 items were removed from the ship and logged under VETS (Vessel Equipment Tracking System). These items were either returned to the MoD stores – such as the unwanted Sea Dart missile systems – or overhauled in BRDL's modern workshops on site or by sub-contractors off site. Having been laid up for five years, a major task was to identify how serviceable the mechanical systems were and surveys proved

ARK dwarfs the dock in which she is being fitted.
(Mike Tazioli, Babcock Engineering Services Ltd)

ARK ROYAL in dry dock in Rosyth.
(Mike Tazioli, Babcock Engineering Services Ltd)

that much of the pipe work and valves were defective. These were either repaired or replaced. While in dry dock the ship's sonar dome was removed for overhaul and replaced and a major survey of the propeller shafts was completed which resulted in three sections being renewed. Also at this stage in the refit two new propellers were fitted, each weighing 26 tonnes – the equivalent of 13 cars – and measuring around 13 ft in diameter, with the main purpose of allowing the ship to move more swiftly through the water. Weld repairs were required on both the starboard and port rudders and the four stabilisers were removed for survey and overhaul. Thousands of valves and hundreds of pumps were removed and overhauled or renewed. Overhauling the gearboxes took six months alone and of the five auxiliary boilers, three were renewed and two overhauled.

ARK ROYAL had arrived without her main engines. Therefore, as soon as she was returned from dry dock to J&K Berth in January 2001, work began on fitting four refurbished Rolls Royce Olympus gas turbines – two port and two starboard – which would provide 112,000 horsepower to propel the ship at speeds of up to 30 knots. Also missing was one of her eight diesel generators that supply electricity to the ship. The remaining generators were removed and the refit involved fitting three new generators and overhauling the other five. The vessel is designed so that every piece of main machinery can be removed and she is fitted with lifts to aid this. In the case of fitting the three-tonne, cylindrical gas turbines, which measure around six ft in diameter and 10 ft long, these were hoisted by a dockside crane down through the aircraft lift apertures and into the hangar deck. From there, the ship's lifts took them to their compartments and, using a combination of beams, chain blocks and rails, they were deposited into their modules which are protected against fire and designed to contain the noise. ARK ROYAL's main machinery space lifts were used daily to remove and replace equipment and, as they are used infrequently while the vessel is operational, BRDL took on the responsibility of their maintenance.

A major mechanical change to the vessel was to fit an additional air conditioning plant and to supply extra chilled water to weapons and accommodation areas, which involved fitting miles of new pipework. Two and a half miles of 8 mm pipework alone were used to install pressure gauges to the fire system and 50 fire fighting hose reels were fitted throughout the vessel.

The 12-month job of removing, overhauling and replacing the two aircraft lifts was a major achievement in itself. The platform of each lift is the size of a tennis court and weighs 28 tonnes. The lifts, one fore and one aft, take the aircraft from the hangar up 30 ft to the flight deck. Massive cranes had to be hired by BRDL to lift the platforms out through their existing apertures in the flight deck from where they were moved by a trailer into the dockyard's Syncrolift building, a huge workshop facility where small ships can be refitted out of water and under cover.

One of the most challenging jobs on board was to prepare the vessel for the operation of the Harrier GR7, a huge construction task that involved attaching a whole new section

The aircraft lifts had to be removed, overhauled and replaced.
(Mike Tazioli, Babcock Engineering Services Ltd)

to the ship's side and flight deck. Fabricators in BRDL's workshops on site fashioned four modules from around 160 tonnes of steel. These were fitted on to the existing structure after the removal of the Sea Dart missile system, which included getting rid of hydraulics, lighting and the missile ramp. This new section created nine compartments: four magazines for GR7 munitions and additional briefing and

The refit has seen ARK ROYAL's flight deck extended and hangar upgraded to fly and accommodate, for the first time from an aircraft carrier, the Merlin anti-submarine warfare helicopter.

planning rooms for Merlin. A weapons lift was also fitted into the newly-vacated space and existing magazines were changed to house the latest armaments.

Around 600 square metres of parking space was provided for the Merlin and GR7 by transforming an unused fo'c's'le area adjacent to the ski ramp into flight deck. Supporting activities on the flight deck are systems and services that operate from the open catwalks which stretch around the ship's stern and up both port and starboard sides. These include fresh water, wash down facilities, fire safety equipment as well as fuelling and defuelling systems. Additional fuel points were fitted so that fuelling and defuelling can take place simultaneously. The main power supplies for the GR7 and Merlin were also updated – a Merlin uses just under 1000 amps alone for starting. In addition, systems were installed for the Merlin to upload and download computer information before and after flights.

The existing catwalks were removed and disposed of and new external walkways were manufactured in 32 modules, again in the dockyard's workshops. While still in dry dock the modules were hoisted on to the ship by cranes before the welders got down to business. Around 12 miles of welding was required on the catwalks alone – almost the distance of a half marathon. Many modifications were made to improve the safety and security of the aircraft while on the platforms, as well as on the flight deck. The GR7 and Merlin are larger and heavier than the previous in-service aircraft and necessitated the fitting of some 1400 securing points to the hangar and flight decks, as well as to the aircraft lift platforms, to keep the aircraft steady while at sea.

Another major addition to the ship's structure was a new Flyco (Flying Control Position). As aircraft take off and come into land they are observed from the Flyco, the equivalent of an airport control tower, which houses three operators. The old Flyco, attached to the compass platform, was cut off and a new compartment fabricated in one piece within the dockyard. The new compartment contains an extra row of windows below the existing ones and new skylight windows were fitted in the deck head (the roof of the compartment) which offer improved visibility of the port side and of aircraft as they land.

One of the main modifications to the aircraft lift platforms involved the locking gear, which secures the platform at flight deck level. Instead of mechanisms locking from the platforms into the flight deck they now lock into the lifts from the flight deck, which gives the platforms more stability. A new anti-tilt mechanism was fitted to the platforms to ensure the lift remains stable when being used.

All aircraft take-off and landing support aids were removed for overhaul or replacement and new CCTV cameras were installed. This also involved the fitting of a new glide path indicator, which guides the aircraft into land. Safety is also crucial on the hangar deck where all the aircraft are maintained and parked. The hangar is about the size of two football pitches placed end-to-end and is divided into three areas by two fire curtains, which were renewed. Hanging the curtains was a challenge for BRDL and an external contractor

The aft hangar during the refit.

was given 10 days to complete the task but needed just seven to get the curtains on board, unroll the heavy-duty material, lay them out and chain block them up and onto a roller.

Several new aviation workshops, which house the latest technology, were constructed and outfitted along with new offices to meet the needs of the GR7 and Merlin crews. Space for spare parts for the aircraft is extremely tight and BRDL was tasked with fitting new shelving around the hangar, a huge task which, when scheduled around other A&As, took around a year to complete. Four gantry cranes were fitted, one fore, two mid and one aft, to lift the heavy spares to and from the shelves, which allow the GR7s to be maintained in the aft section of the ship. Locating the fixed wing aircraft near the aft lift will simplify operations on the hangar and flight decks. The hangar and flight decks were made to look like new again thanks to the renewal of the non-skid paint system. The old paint was taken off first using a combination of high pressure water blasting and blast-tracks before the new coatings were sprayed on. Painters got through around 2951 litres of paint on the flight deck – the equivalent of 1180 tins of household paint – and the hangar deck took 1648 litres, the equivalent of 660 tins.

An important addition to the ship, which came about later in the refit, was the installation of a gaseous liquid oxygen making plant to provide the pilots of the fixed wing aircraft with air. Modern aircraft can make oxygen on board but the Sea Harrier can't so the ship has to produce it or store it. Extremely high safety standards were demanded when installing the machinery as liquid oxygen is highly explosive. As a back-up to this equipment, should it fail, another piece of machinery was installed that stores oxygen and pumps it up to the required pressure for the pilots' air tanks.

Towering over the flight deck, between ARK ROYAL's fore and aft funnels, is her main mast which houses some of the ship's radar, communication and electronic warfare equipment and antennas. For operational and structural reasons the old mast had to be completely replaced. All systems, both on the mast and below deck, were dismantled and the structure was basically cut off at the bottom and taken away in sections. Meanwhile BRDL rose to the challenge of constructing a new, 18.5 metre high mast. The structure was manufactured in three modules in the Dockyard's workshops, in the space of 10 weeks, and then transported to the

Work progresses on the refit.

Progress on the refit is surveyed by FOSNNI on a visit to Rosyth Dockyard.

Both galleys were stripped back to the bare bones and new cabling, linings and high-tech equipment were fitted.

Syncrolift building where it was assembled into one piece and lifted onto the ship by a massive crane on the dockside.

With the removal of the Sea Dart missile system, ARK ROYAL's remaining self-defence system is the fast reaction, rapid fire Phalanx gun, which is located in three positions on the ship in the fore, mid and aft sections. The midship Phalanx gun had to be moved up a deck to make room for a decoy launcher on the starboard side, however the fore and aft guns remain in their original positions. The refit contract included an extensive package of work to bring the ship's office and accommodation areas up to a high standard to meet the needs of the men and women serving in the Royal Navy in the new millennium. BRDL was presented with a huge task but one in which everyone, from project managers to tradesmen, took immense pride. The challenge came in having to complete 463 of the ship's total 1228 compartments by the deadline of 30 March 2001, the day 400 of the ship's staff moved on board.

Many of the ship's systems, such as fresh water and air conditioning, had to be up and running for this date and BRDL had to adopt different ways of working to achieve this, while still keeping up to date with refitting the remaining compartments. However, the deadline was met and from that date there was a particularly strong spirit of co-operation between the Ship's Company and BRDL to have all ARK ROYAL's systems and services completely operational and to complete the refit on time and to the highest standards.

The ship was fitted with five new sewage treatment

plants, two fore, one mid and two aft, there was a major upgrade of fridges and cool rooms and an additional fridge storeroom provided. All equipment in the laundry was removed and replaced with up-to-date washing machines, presses and irons. The dental surgery, laboratory and sick bay were also fully upgraded.

The ship has 68 air treatment units to provide warm and cool air, which were also overhauled and operational in time for the ship's staff moving on board. The 'dry' areas, such as mess decks (recreation areas), dining halls and sleeping quarters, were extensively refurbished to a common standard of finish, whether for ratings or officers. Many were fitted out with new furniture, such as tables, chairs, lockers and bunks, as well as new decking and carpets, wall linings, ceilings and soft furnishings.

ARK has two galleys, the main galley and the officers' galley, which are a hive of activity when it comes to feeding the Ship's Company of 1100 men and women. Both galleys were stripped back to the bare bones and wasted sections of the steel decks cut away and renewed before new cabling, linings and high-tech equipment were fitted. The ship's catering staff now have the most efficient of appliances at their fingertips. These include, in the main galley, three 80-litre tilting kettles, five combination ovens that can fit 10 dishes and five with space for six, two 80-litre pans, one 40-litre pan, three deep fat fryers, a slicer, a food processor and, for storing the food, two large fridges. A food preparation area also contains a large fridge and a freezer, a food mixer, a cutter/mixer, two potato peeling machines and a garbage disposal unit.

All living and office quarters are protected by a state of the art fire detection system. A total of 612 sensors were fitted throughout the ship and as soon as one goes off its precise location can be immediately pinpointed. Extra 230-volt electrical sockets were also fitted to office and living spaces to allow personnel to use equipment such as televisions, video recorders and stereo systems, as well as personal electrical equipment. BRDL called upon the talents of the craftsmen and women in Babcock Joinery to furnish some quarters. Probably their most impressive achievement was the manufacture of a new bar, made from ash wood, that stretches the length of the refurbished Wardroom.

ARK ROYAL received a major upgrade of its weapons and sensors as well as its internal and external communications. At the heart of this is the Command Support System (CSS), which communicates with both shore

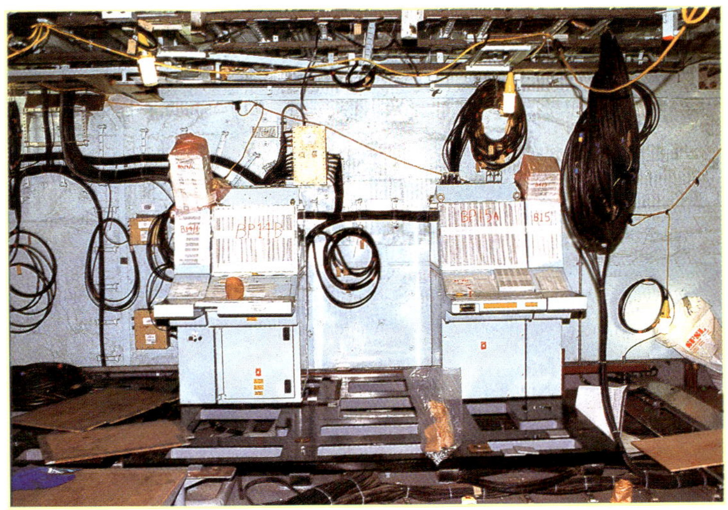

The Operations Room was stripped of all its display equipment for renewal or overhaul.

headquarters and other platforms via dedicated interfaces and also receives a tactical picture from the command system or over data links. The ship was also equipped with NSSA (Naval Sector Strategic Architecture). This is a network of workstations that supports the medium to long-term planning needs of the ship, for example stores, and provides an interface with shore headquarters and other platforms. Around 16 miles of cabling alone was used to fit the 140 workstations with computers, processors and, in most cases, printers.

A lengthy 22 miles of cabling was wired between the computer room and the Operations Room – the main command centre for the ship's weapons – which was stripped of all its display equipment for renewal or overhaul. The floating steel rafts, on which the equipment is sited for stability, were removed to the Dockyard's workshops for modification to suit the new layout of the room. BRDL constructed a new Force Operations Room and Flag Main Communications Office and a new Flag Planning Room was redesigned and installed with the CSS. The Special Intelligence Office also received extensive upgrading to carry the latest equipment. The Main Communications Office was stripped and extensively rewired in preparation for a new layout and new equipment. A new automatic message handling system was installed as well as SCOT, the latest satellite communications system. The ship now also carries the latest electronic warfare equipment. ARK ROYAL was fitted to provide a Joint Forces Headquarters (JFHQ). The refit included a 'fit to receive' JFHQ package to redesignate specific compartments and enhance and improve external and internal communications, including the installation of CNN satellite news. The main areas of the JFHQ would consist of the Admiral's Dining Cabin, the Wardroom Ante Room and the guest room, which were fitted with concealed internal communications systems.

State of the art radars for navigation, surveillance, pilotage and helicopter operations were fitted to ARK ROYAL. out of date radars, antennas and electrical equipment were removed first before the new equipment was installed and new office space created. Aerials that had been fitted to the old main mast were relocated on the funnels and the new foremast yardarms, the ship's sonar equipment was modified and the transducer – the equipment for transmitting and receiving signals – renewed.

Achievement of the originally planned SSMOB (Ships Staff Move on Board) date was a huge milestone as the 'hotel' side of the vessel, including all relevant systems, had to be commissioned and the ship certified ready for habitation by 400 Royal Navy personnel, many of them new recruits. This milestone coincided with the visit to ARK ROYAL by the Secretary of State for Defence, Geoff Hoon, who witnessed the tremendous teamwork of Royal Navy, Ministry of Defence and Dockyard personnel. During the time that ARK was at Rosyth, working relationships were firmly established between ship's staff, WSA and BRDL personnel, which was to prove a major advantage when difficulties arose and teamwork was required. In particular, the Executive Officer, Lieutenant Commander Glen MacDonald and the Senior Marine Engineer, Lieutenant Commander Bob Graham, who arrived at Rosyth with ARK ROYAL in May 1999 and remained throughout the refit period, were both proven to be firm allies in the sometimes daunting task of awakening the ship from her long sleep. There were many times when BRDL relied on ship's staff for support and this was always forthcoming to ensure that the best interests of ARK ROYAL were considered.

ARK ROYAL has been returned to her original, gleaming glory thanks to the renewal of her superstructure, weather decks, flight deck and hangar deck paint systems. She was moved to the Entrance Lock in July 2001 and, from there, sailed out of Rosyth Dockyard for sea trials before making a scheduled return to the Dockyard in August for an inclining experiment to check her stability. While the ship's staff enjoyed their summer leave BRDL carried out all required repairs to defects that showed up during the trials before ARK ROYAL sailed south on 29 August 2001 for weapons and aircraft trials. BRDL formally handed her back to the Ministry of Defence in the first week of November 2001 and she rejoined the Fleet a week later.

Merlin embarks on ARK ROYAL for the first time on 14 July 2001.

5 POST REFIT

ARK ROYAL has emerged from her extensive refit almost as a new ship. Much work has been carried out to modernise and replace many of the original parts and she has been fitted with the very latest equipment available to the Royal Navy. The majority of the Ship's Company joined ARK during the final stages of the refit and was therefore not familiar with how she looked at the beginning, or, indeed, in her previous commission. This chapter summarises the roles of the ship's individual departments and concludes with a list of affiliations that ARK ROYAL maintains with various organisations.

ARK ROYAL is like new after her extensive refit at Rosyth Dockyard.

HRH The Duke of York marked the end of his naval career with a visit to ARK ROYAL.

Warfare Department

HMS ARK ROYAL's key operational capabilities are:

- The projection of up to 24 aircraft for specified operations anywhere in the world. The Air Group can be tailored, depending on the political requirement, and may include Sea Harriers (FA2), RAF Harriers (GR7), Merlin (Anti-Submarine), Sea King (Airborne Early Warning), Chinook and all other military helicopters.

- The provision of command, control, communications, computer, intelligence and information facilities for maritime, joint and combined operations.

- The support of joint, combined and amphibious operations through the deployment of support helicopters, troops and equipment in the Landing Platform (Helicopter) (LPH)/Fast Dash Role.

- The projection of non-operational aspects of British foreign policy objectives including trading interests.

- Peace support operations and aid to civil power including disaster relief.

These capabilities required some major changes to ARK ROYAL during the refit. By far the most visible change was the removal of the Sea Dart surface to air missile system and its associated Fire Control Radar 909, the famous white domes. This has allowed the flight deck to be extended over the fo'c's'le and for the original Sea Dart magazine to be converted to store munitions and stores primarily for the RAF's Harrier GR7. This means the ship is now able to embark and operate this aircraft more effectively and with greater flexibility. The flight deck and hangar have also received extensive changes to enable ARK to operate the Navy's latest helicopter, the Merlin. The Merlin itself will provide a quantum leap in the Royal Navy's anti-submarine capabilities.

The fitting of the Link 16 Data Link System, to supplement Link II, will provide ARK with an accurate, long range, real time, secure tactical picture provided by an amalgamation of information from her own sensors with that of other ships and aircraft.

The Command Support System (CSS), now fitted in the operations room, allows faster dissemination of tactical information and orders both between separate units and also units and their HQs. This provides a more efficient and reliable method of exercising command and control over a task group.

Executive Department

ARK ROYAL has a Ship's Company of 650, which rises to over 1200 with embarked aircrew and flag staffs. Such a large organisation requires constant administration, which is co-ordinated by the Executive Department. This includes three Service Police Officers, two Physical Training Instructors and the Seamanship sub-department which is responsible for boats, refuelling-at-sea arrangements, life-saving equipment and all other aspects of safety at sea.

Air Department

As mentioned earlier, one of the main changes to ARK's Flight Deck has been the removal of the Sea Dart Guided Missile system in order to allow for more magazine space to accommodate the RAF Harrier GR7 and its associated weapons. This has also allowed for the creation of an extra helicopter take-off and landing spot (Zero Spot) forward of the superstructure. This is needed to offset the loss of two spots on the aft end of the flight deck due to the increased size of the Merlin. In another major change to the flight deck, most of the eye plates have been replaced by more heavy duty ones and their positions moved, again to allow for the difference in weight and size between the Merlin and the older Sea King. A new 'cat walk', a well three ft below the level of the deck, has been built around the flight deck allowing easier movement both around and on and off the flight deck. ARK is the first CVS to have a catwalk around the stern as well as both sides.

The services available to the aircraft spots have all been upgraded with each now receiving their own fuel, water and electrical supplies. This allows a quicker turnaround time (ie the time between landing and taking off again) when the ship is involved in multiple aircraft moves. ARK's night flying capabilities have been enhanced with the fitting of Electro Luminescent Boards to 5 Spot to allow pilots to take-off and land while using Night Vision Goggles (NVG).

Aircraft Weapons and Sensors

Sea Harrier FA2:
AMRAAM – advanced medium range air-to-air missile
Sidewinder – short range missile to be replaced by ASRAAM (advanced short range air-to-air missile)
30 mm Aden Cannon
500 lb and 1,000 lb bombs
Blue Vixen Radar.

Harrier GR7:
Sidewinder anti-air missile
Paveway guided bombs
500 lb and 1,000 lb bombs

Merlin:
Stingray Torpedoes
Mark II Depth Charges
Blue Kestral Radar

Sea King AEW:
No weapons
Searchwater Radar

Meteorological Services

In refit ARK ROYAL has seen the Met Office move from its old position of 1 deck to 01 deck, enabling several changes to be made. Most noticeable is the new window that juts out over the flight deck and allows a greater field of view. The new office is larger and houses more equipment. Along with the standard equipment fit of HF Fax, RATT, AUASS and 4JKA, there have been additions such as the upgraded CSS version 5, which included the Environmental Support Applications, and CLX Message Handling System. Eventually there will be provision for Internet access and a dedicated Mentor satellite telephone line.

All these changes and improvements mean that, once

fully operational, the Met Office in HMS ARK ROYAL will lead the way in 'out of area' and 'at sea' forecasting, as it will be able to receive the same quality and quantity of data from worldwide sources as you would expect to find at a Met Office ashore.

Air Engineering Department

The hangar has changed significantly in the refit. A new shelf, three metres wide by five metres high, has been built on the port side midships to accommodate the sizeable stores for Merlin along with a two-metre wide shelf that goes almost the entire way around the hangar. A total of 1200 new linkplates, complete with new lashings, have been installed into the hangar and flight decks. This has taken an inordinate amount of time due to the additional work required to prepare the area of weld. In addition, a new concept of storage has been introduced for the first time on CVS class ships, called 'Modular Support', in which the majority of tools and equipment for aircraft maintenance are now stored in the same boxes ashore as used afloat. This will undoubtedly save a great deal of time for the transportation of equipment. Prior to the refit only one overhead gantry was fitted, now an additional three cover virtually the entire hangar to allow movement of stores to and from the shelves.

The Merlin.

A CVS hangar is divided into three sections – forward, centre and aft – by 'fire curtains' which can be dropped in the event of a fire to prevent it spreading. There is also a remotely operated spray system so that any fire that affects the whole hangar can be quickly extinguished. The traditional layout of the hangar has also changed, with the Sea Harrier and GR7 now at the rear and the Merlin at the forward end. The improved Sea King Mk 7 will be in the centre hangar section. The hangar is also the 'at sea' home for the ship's Jaguar Sovereign car, kindly on loan from Jaguar to promote overseas sales.

In contrast to previous RN helicopters, Merlin relies heavily on complex IT systems within the aircraft and therefore the ship has required a great deal of specific computer support to be fitted.

ARK has all the maintenance equipment and personnel to carry out the vast majority of routine maintenance and defect rectification required for all its aircraft types while at sea. This does entail the serviceable aircraft being stowed on the flight deck though in order to make room.

Merlin inside the hangar.

Marine Engineering Department

ARK ROYAL's propulsion system is divided between four main machinery spaces – two engine rooms and two gear rooms. Main propulsion power is provided by four Rolls-Royce Marine Olympus gas turbines from the same family as the engines fitted to Concorde, each producing 25,000bhp. The engines drive two bi-directional shafts through the largest reversing gearboxes installed in any ship in the western world. When manoeuvring ahead or astern, the drive is transmitted via fluid couplings but, for higher efficiency in the ahead direction only, the drive is transmitted via syncro-self-shifting clutches. Designed and built by David Brown Limited, these gearboxes allow any number of engines to be coupled in (two per shaft) to drive the ship at the required speed. Electrical power, sufficient to light a modest sized town, is provided by eight Paxman Valenta diesel generators, similar to those used in high-speed trains, while large distilling plants and reverse osmosis plants make fresh water for domestic use.

Engineering – a never ending task.

During the refit all major items of machinery were overhauled to ensure the ship is fully equipped for forthcoming operational requirements and a large number of alterations and modifications were also carried out to bring equipment to the most up to date levels of performance.

Machinery is operated, monitored and maintained by a highly trained team of marine engineers, technicians and mechanics comprising six Officers, 50 Chief Petty Officers and Petty Officers and 90 Junior Ratings.

Weapon Engineering Department

The ship's weapons include three 20 mm Phalanx Close-in Weapon Systems (CIWS), two 20 mm Gambo Close Range guns and five General Purpose Machine-Guns (GPMG). The ship's sensors are:

1022 Long Range Early Warning Radar

Radar 1022 is the Royal Navy's long range surveillance radar. The system is integrated into the existing Action Data Automation Weapons Systems (ADAWS) and therefore does not include display units. It entered service in the late 1980s and replaced the older Radar 965. It is synchronised from an external source and uses a travelling wave tube to generate a frequency modulated composite pulse to detect both air and surface targets at a range of up to 220 nautical miles.

Setting to work ARK's Phalanx point defence systems.

996 Medium Range Target Indication Radar

Fitted to CVS, Type 42 and Type 23 ships, Radar Type 996 is a three-dimensional naval surveillance and target indication radar that gives:

Wide vertical coverage
Multi-role operation
Extensive ECCM
Automatic initiation and tracking
Matched to weapon systems
Proven operation
A range of 90 to 100 nautical miles.

1007 Navigational Radar

Radar 1007 is an I-band system designed for navigation, blind pilotage, surface surveillance and helicopter control.

Primary role:
Ship's safety and collision avoidance

Secondary roles:
High definition surface warning
Manoeuvring
Station keeping
Blind pilotage
Aid to navigation
Small craft control
Helicopter control

Performance:
For an antenna not less that 40 ft from the water, the set should have a 50 per cent chance of detecting a small contact, such as a danbuoy reflector, at not less than seven miles.

1008 Navigational Radar

Radar 1008 is a civilian standard E/F band radar used solely for navigation. It gives enhanced detection of surface contacts, enabling early warning of shipping in any visibility. It is a 'stand alone' piece of equipment fitted immediately forward of, and providing information to, the bridge

2016 Search Sonar

Sonar 2016 is a hull-mounted medium range active Sonar. Fitted with its own dedicated computer, 2016 uses digital techniques to detect and track multiple underwater targets in the active mode and has a passive torpedo warning capability.

Supply and Secretariat Department

Accommodation

The standard complement of the ARK is 656 of which 60 are Officers. With an embarked air group of up to 366 (80 Officers) this gives a total of almost 1100, of which 140 are Officers. In addition, joint staffs may embark, increasing numbers even further. In the event of the need to embark additional staff for joint or combined operations, the maximum number of available bunks is:

Male Junior Rates	573
Female Junior Rates	141
Male Petty Officers	162
Male WOs and Chief Petty Officers	139
Female Senior Rates	12
Officers	207
Total	1234

Galley

The galley has the capacity to feed around 1200 people, four times a day (when necessary), and can be manned around the clock, whether at sea or alongside. The ship makes its own bread every night at sea to ensure the Ship's Company awakes to the smell of fresh bread. Food services areas comprise the main galley, the Wardroom galley, the Captain's (VIPs) galley and the bakery. A separate 'fast food' area, the Aircrew Refreshment Bar (ACRB), provides personnel, who are unable to dine at the normal times due to flying commitments, with essential rations. The main and wardroom galleys have been totally refurbished and an extra fridge fitted.

Wardroom

Up to 207 Officers of mixed rank and gender can be accommodated in the Wardroom. The Wardroom dining room, bar and ante room have been totally refurbished during refit. The Captain's and VIP quarters, and the Bridge Mess, have also been refurbished.

The main change to the Wardroom is that it has also been fitted out to embark a Joint Force Headquarters (JFHQ). This consists of easily removable ceiling panels with ports for communications equipment, etc, to plug straight into the ship's supplies. Similarly, the VIP quarters have been included in this. Although this means the loss of the use of the Wardroom ante room and the VIP quarters for the duration of JFHQ's time on board, it facilitates the smooth embarkation of a large battle staff in a short period of time and confirms the modern role of a CVS as a command platform.

The galleys can be a hive of activity around the clock.

Stores

The stores department carried out a full re-store after the refit, a programme that was started over two years beforehand. There are in excess of 30,000 storeroom stock items on board, with departmental requirements of around 20,000 per year, and these are stored in 14 storerooms plus the hangar. Most departments hold their own stocks rather than one central holding. The stores sub-department supports the Warfare, Air, ME, WE and Medical departments. The scope of stores required by the ship ranges from pencils to spare Olympus gas turbine engines and from 'pussers' black socks to laser guided bombs for the Harrier GR7.

The stores staff comprises one Officer, one WO, two CPO(SA)s, four PO(SA)s, four LSAs and 10 SAs. Replenishment is varied. ARK can Replenish At Sea (RAS) with an RFA by either Vertrep (helicopter) or Jackstay, or dual loads by Vertrep and Jackstay. Return alongside after only three or four weeks away can generate up to 30 pallets to re-store. For example INVINCIBLE, on returning from an eight-month deployment, came home to more than 300 pallets in order to re-store the ship.

The ship's chefs create tasty meals.

Medical and Chaplaincy Services

The medical department on board ARK is routinely staffed as an extended general practice and is equipped as a small hospital. There are consulting rooms, a pharmacy and a ward for the more serious illnesses. The modern operating theatre is available for routine minor surgery and emergency surgery when a surgical team is embarked. A separate dental surgery, with all the facilities of a modern dental practice, is also available.

HMS ARK ROYAL has a Chaplain permanently embarked whose primary purpose is to promote the spiritual and pastoral wellbeing of the entire Ship's Company. This means that, in addition to conducting services and attending to people's spiritual needs, as any priest or minister in a civilian setting would do, the Chaplain has the key role of 'friend and

The Interactive Learning Centre.

advisor to all on board', from the Captain to the youngest sailor, irrespective of religious belief. This often involves working in partnership with the Divisional System and other support agencies to ensure that personnel get the best and most appropriate care and support available. The Chaplain makes a unique contribution in being able to offer complete and unconditional confidentiality in all dealings with personnel. As most of a Chaplain's work is non-denominational, all 'front-line' appointments can be filled by a Chaplain from any of the major Christian faiths. When a specific denominational need exists, or one relating to another of the major 'world faiths', it is the Chaplain's responsibility to make appropriate arrangements to meet this. When a full Air Group is embarked, a visiting Air Group Chaplain may accompany it to work in partnership with the Ship's Chaplain in providing for the needs of the whole ship.

Affiliations

ARK ROYAL has current and active affiliations with the following groups and organisations:

The Queen's Royal Lancers (QRL)

This affiliation was originally established in 1985, as ARK was coming out of build, with the 17th/21st Lancers which subsequently amalgamated with another regiment to become the Queen's Royal Lancers. The QRL is an Armoured Regiment recently converted to operating the latest Challenger 2 tank. Over the years there have been many events to promote this affiliation, including medium term loan drafts, ship visits, sporting events and regimental band playing at various ARK ROYAL social events. Towards the end of the refit the affiliation was re-established with members of the regiment joining the ship on the transit to Portsmouth.

Worshipful Company of Shipwrights
City of Leeds
Headingley Royal Naval Association
Yorkshire Fleet Air Arm Association
Leeds Branch RN Historic Flight Group
Leeds United FC

St Andrews Golf Club

HMS ARK ROYAL's Golf Society has a long standing liaison with St Andrews Golf Club, one of the many clubs based in and around the town of St Andrews, Fife. This very social affiliation was maintained throughout the ship's years in extended readiness from 1995-1999 when parties of golfers from the ship regularly travelled to St Andrews from Portsmouth. More recently, with the ship in refit at Rosyth Dockyard, Fife, the Society has found it easier to maintain the liaison and friendly matches have been played both at St Andrews and on a return basis at Pitreavie Golf Club in Dunfermline. Many of the club members have become good friends and this popular and friendly liaison culminated in members being taken to sea on board ARK ROYAL for the day on 31 July 2001.

Wartime Ark Royal Association

This association has long standing ties with ARK ROYAL IV and V and had its 60th anniversary dinner on board on 13 November 2001.

Jaguar Cars

ARK's ties with Jaguar cars were re-established during the refit. Jaguar has loaned ARK a Long Wheel Base Sovereign car (in British Racing Green) on an annual basis which is used not only for the ship's benefit but also to promote British Industry, especially when the ship is overseas. The car was collected in May 2001 and the Captain visited Jaguar at Allesley, Coventry in June.

The hangar also serves as a sports facility for whole ship events.

ARK's first day off Rosyth after the refit on 13 July 2001.

Fifty Fund

The Fifty Fund is a charity which re-commissions old locomotives. It is currently working on 50035 Ark Royal and was hoping to re-dedicate it at the same time as ARK's re-dedication on 22 November 2001. A previous Captain of Ark Royal IV attended the train's last dedication in 1979 and the affiliation has recently been re-established.

Sea Cadet Corps and Combined Cadet Forces

Leeds SCC (TS Ark Royal)
Reigate SCC (TS Ark Royal)
Marlow SCC (TS Apollo)
Shirley Solihull SCC (TS Gamecock)
St Johns School CCF (Leatherhead)
Kings College School CCF (Wimbledon)

Helicopter operations started early during trials in July 2001.

The Red Arrows

ARK has recently commenced an affiliation with the Royal Air Force Aerobatic Team (RAFAT), more commonly known as the Red Arrows.

The Ship's Company, joined by workers from Rosyth Dockyard, formed this birthday message for Her Majesty The Queen Mother.

6 THE FUTURE

ARK ROYAL rejoins a fleet in which the aircraft carrier has regained its position as being as central to the capabilities of the Royal Navy as it was the carrier heyday of the 1950s and 60s. The Strategic Defence Review (SDR) of 1998 stated that: "The focus of our maritime forces in the new environment will move towards rapid deployment operations." In these scenarios carriers "would have a wide utility, including deterrence and coercion." The lessons of the 1990s had been well and truly learned. In the messy strategic contexts of the 1990s, the ability to bring to bear air power from a mobile, national base, not subject to the vagaries of host nation support or the uncertainties of the situation ashore, had been vindicated on numerous occasions. In the Adriatic ARK ROYAL's remaining 'poised to protect' UNPROFOR in general, and BRITFOR in particular, was a perfect demonstration of the dynamics of post Cold War naval air power.

Operation Palliser, British intervention in Sierra Leone, vindicated the accuracy of the SDR's analysis where carrier capability once again proved vital. Carriers are now accepted as the single most important component of Britain's new expeditionary strategy, adding strategic weight by their mere presence. The carriers complement the UK's amphibious ready group that is itself in a process of highly significant modernisation. Together, the Royal Navy's power projection forces provide the maritime capability for joint operations that is at the heart of contemporary maritime and defence doctrine.

The key word is 'joint', for ARK ROYAL will henceforward carry a joint RN/RAF Carrier Air Group known as a Tailored Air Group (TAG). Another initiative of the SDR, and a vital part of the carrier case, was the merging, on 1 April 2000, of the Royal Navy's Sea Harriers and the RAF's GR7 Harriers in 'Joint Force Harrier' (JFH), the means by which the new concept of 'Joint Force 2000' will be brought to fruition. That will see four squadrons of the new Future Joint Combat Aircraft operating from two new large carriers, over twice the size of ARK ROYAL. In the meantime 800 and 801 squadrons now form part of JFH together with three RAF Harrier squadrons. JFH, together with the Nimrod maritime patrol aircraft and the RAF's air sea rescue helicopters, now form 3 Group RAF.

Sea trials in July 2001, still with boats on the Flight Deck!

The first Merlin landing on deck on 14 July 2001 (left).

The commander is a Rear Admiral with a fully joint staff at RAF Strike Command headquarters.

Joint Force Harrier's mission is: "To provide a force, able to deploy from land and sea, capable of precision attack on land, sea and air targets, able to undertake timely reconnaissance, and air escort of Joint and Allied assets to support the Joint Commander's Directive in pursuit of UK Defence aims across the spectrum of peace, crisis and conflict."

The two types of aircraft available to JFH offer a set of complementary capabilities that mesh together well to fulfil this mission. The Sea Harrier FA2s, of which one squadron of eight will normally deploy in ARK on a permanent basis, are still avionically the most advanced fighters in Europe in the air-to-air mode with the Blue Vixen radar for beyond visual range engagements with AMRAAM (Advanced Medium Range Air-to-Air Missile). For shorter range work the proven AIM-9 Sidewinder is to be replaced with ASRAAM (Advanced Short Range Air-to-Air Missile). The FA2 also carries an even more proven weapon, the 30 mm cannon, that has a multiplicity of uses as a weapon of more limited force in both air-to-air and air-to-ground situations. In the attack mode the aircraft can carry 1,000 lb or 540 lb bombs and in the reconnaissance role the aircraft is fitted with a simple internal F95 camera, a capability that has proven most useful in numerous operations with the SHAR.

For serious air-to-ground work ARK would normally embark a squadron of GR7s. These are more advanced than the SHARs in terms of their airframes and unlike the SHARs have a night ground attack capability. They can carry the same bombs as the SHAR but can designate laser-guided versions, dropped either from themselves or other aircraft. The GR7s can also carry Maverick television guided missiles for precision attack.

ARK ROYAL gives a mix of up to 16 of these aircraft a secure, mobile base for sustained operations with excellent command and control facilities. It can operate day or night, and high sortie generation rates mean that much can be obtained from a relatively small number of aircraft. The main operational problem in the near future is the problem of vertical landing with bombs attached in very hot conditions. This will be solved when the improved GR9, with its uprated engine, replaces the GR7 between 2003 and 2007.

When ARK operates with a full JFH air group her normal complement of helicopters will be up to six, four Airborne Early Warning Sea Kings and two Merlin ASW aircraft. The venerable AEW2s are about to be replaced with the AEW7, electronically as advanced as any airborne early warning aircraft in the world with an excellent capability over both land and sea.

Merlin offers a parallel step improvement in capability. It can lay claim to being the most advanced maritime helicopter in the world. Its Blue Kestrel radar, with a sophisticated processing suite, offers an ability to carry out wide area surface surveillance and targeting over the entire littoral. The long range sonar suite, with both sonobuoys and the highly capable AQS 960 dipping set, doubles the capability in the old Sea King ASW fleet and will make the life of even the quietest enemy submarine far more hazardous than most submariners would like. The helicopter can carry Stingray homing torpedoes or depth charges if it is appropriate to take on the contact itself.

Both types of helicopter together provide a major new capacity as 'battlespace shapers', providing information to the joint force commander as to the nature of his environment and where he might have to direct his weapons. They have the ability to network their information through Data Links 16 and 11. Merlin goes to sea in ARK for the first time in the shape of four aircraft from 814 Squadron, which will be increased to six as more airframes become available.

Normally ARK will carry all of them along with her allocated SHAR squadron and the AEW flight; deployment of the GR7s would mean most Merlins going to other ships in the force, such as Royal Fleet Auxiliaries. The advantage of the carrier is its flexibility. The air group can be mixed and matched according to task. For an evacuation operation, for example, Commando Sea Kings or other assets of the new Joint Helicopter Force might well take up some or even all of the aircraft space on board. The commissioning of the amphibious transport helicopter carrier LPH HMS Ocean means that there is now a dedicated platform for transport helicopter duties but a ship with a flight deck can do many things, as required.

ARK ROYAL might well have an even more key role in addition to operating whatever aircraft the situation requires. Her refit allows her to act as the forward deployed Joint Force Headquarters itself. It might not be possible, particularly in the early stages of a crisis deployment, to have this ashore and now the ship is fitted for the rapid insertion of a fully fledged JFHQ with enough space for the required Officers and their staffs and enough communications for the increasingly network-centric operations of tomorrow.

In all, the new refitted ARK ROYAL will be one of the most important single assets available to British Governments as they continue their expeditionary and maritime strategy of making the United Kingdom a 'force for good' on a global scale in a highly uncertain world. In a globalised international system where combined international action is becoming more and more the rule, she could make a major complementary contribution to a NATO or US-led force. Alternatively, she might herself lead a European Union peace support operation. Any maritime task group, of which she would inevitably be a major part, will have "the ability to project, sustain and apply effective military force from the sea, at global range in order to influence, modify or change events on land". Adopting the maritime approach offers the advantages of sea basing, that is protection, mobility, and an afloat logistical infrastructure based in the world's most efficient transport medium. Maritime Task Groups can deploy early, can poise as the situation clarifies and do not require host nation support. No wonder they are the core of current defence policy and are likely to remain so as long as ARK ROYAL remains in service.

Merlin taking off (right).

ARK ROYAL has a decade or so of active life in front of her and can expect one more rather less intensive refit to allow her to remain in service through to 2015, by which time the two new carriers will be in service. Even then her service may not be over. The Royal Navy has still not given up on the idea of a second LPH to add to its amphibious force. ARK ROYAL, as the youngest of the present carriers, is considered a suitable and cost-effective candidate. There may very well be several more books to mark the recommissioning or rededication of the Royal Navy's most famous ship, HMS ARK ROYAL.

585

83 RN 61
585

Merlin (left) trying the forward lift for size and (above) ARK ROYAL during post refit trials.

THANK YOU

Our thanks go to all those who contributed in the production of this book and to the following companies from the City of Leeds which kindly donated funds to assist with the rededication day on 22 November 2001.

Leeds Co-Operative Society Limited

IMI Yorkshire Fittings Limited

Pinset Curtis Charitable Trust

Sulzer Pumps (UK) Limited